Image-makers of Kumortuli and the Durga Puja Festival

Image-makers of Kumortuli and the Durga Puja Festival

Krishna Dutta

NIYOGI
BOOKS

Published by

NIYOGI BOOKS

D-78, Okhla Industrial Area, Phase-I
New Delhi-110 020, INDIA
Tel: 91-11-26816301, 49327000
Fax: 91-11-26810483, 26813830
Email: niyogibooks@gmail.com
Website: www.niyogibooksindia.com

Editor: Soma Das / Upama Biswas
Design: Nabanita Das

ISBN: 978-93-85285-13-4
Publication: 2016
Reprint: 2026

Printed at: Niyogi Offset Pvt. Ltd., New Delhi, India

For Ariadne, a loyal friend and a regular visitor to Kolkata, and admirers of the spirit of the place all over the world.

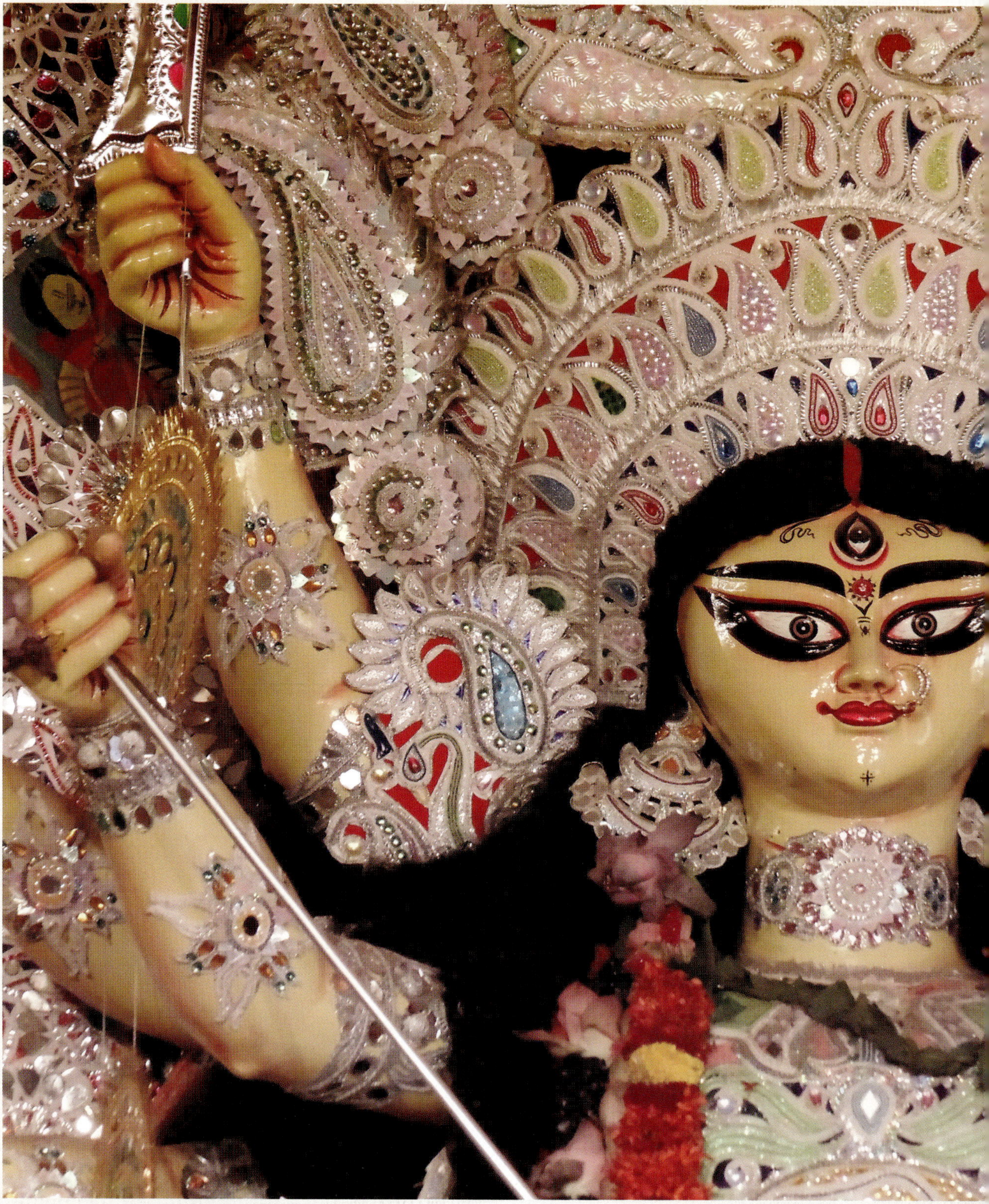

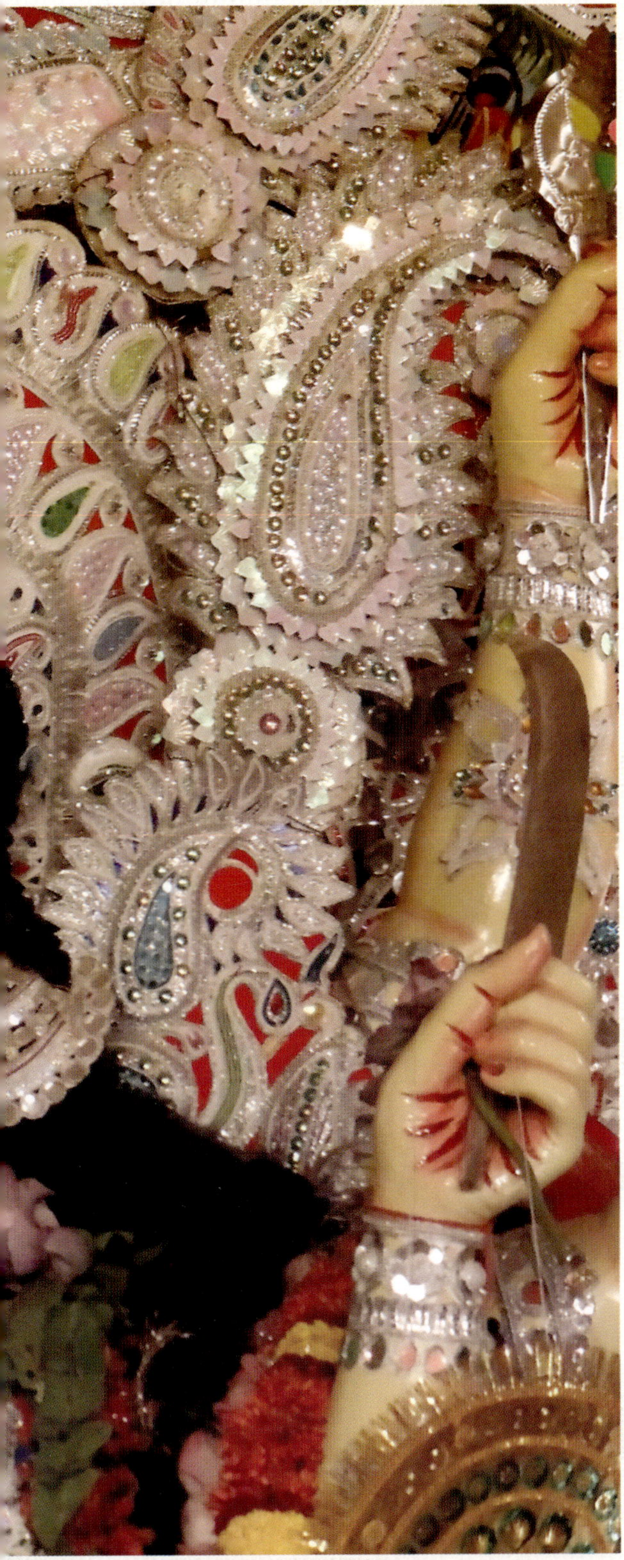

Contents

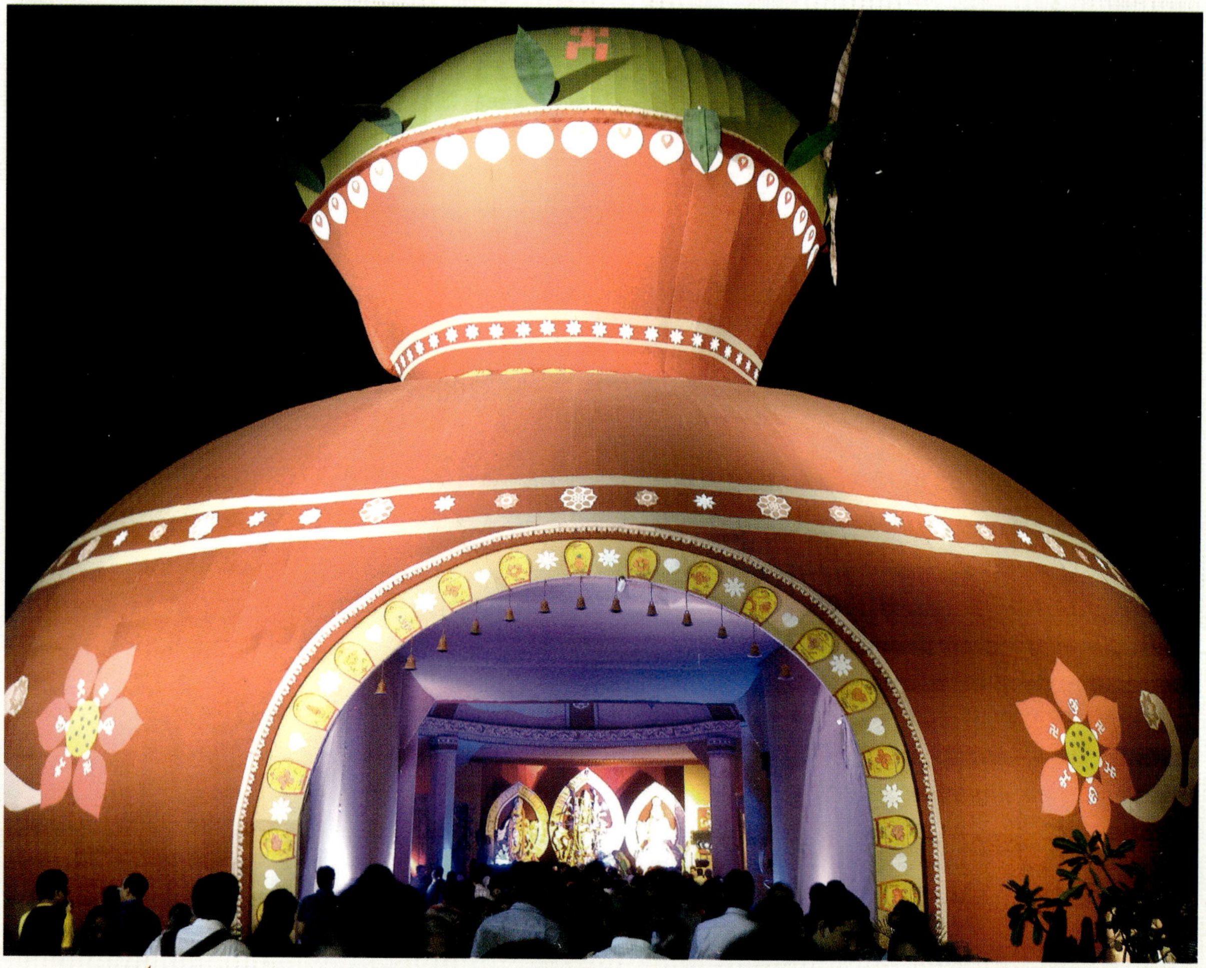

The ubiquitous *ghot* of Hindu rituals as a pandal concept during Durga Puja (courtesy: Siddhartha Banerjee)

Pages 6-7: The all-seeing third eye of Goddess Durga (courtesy: Nabanita Das)

Introduction

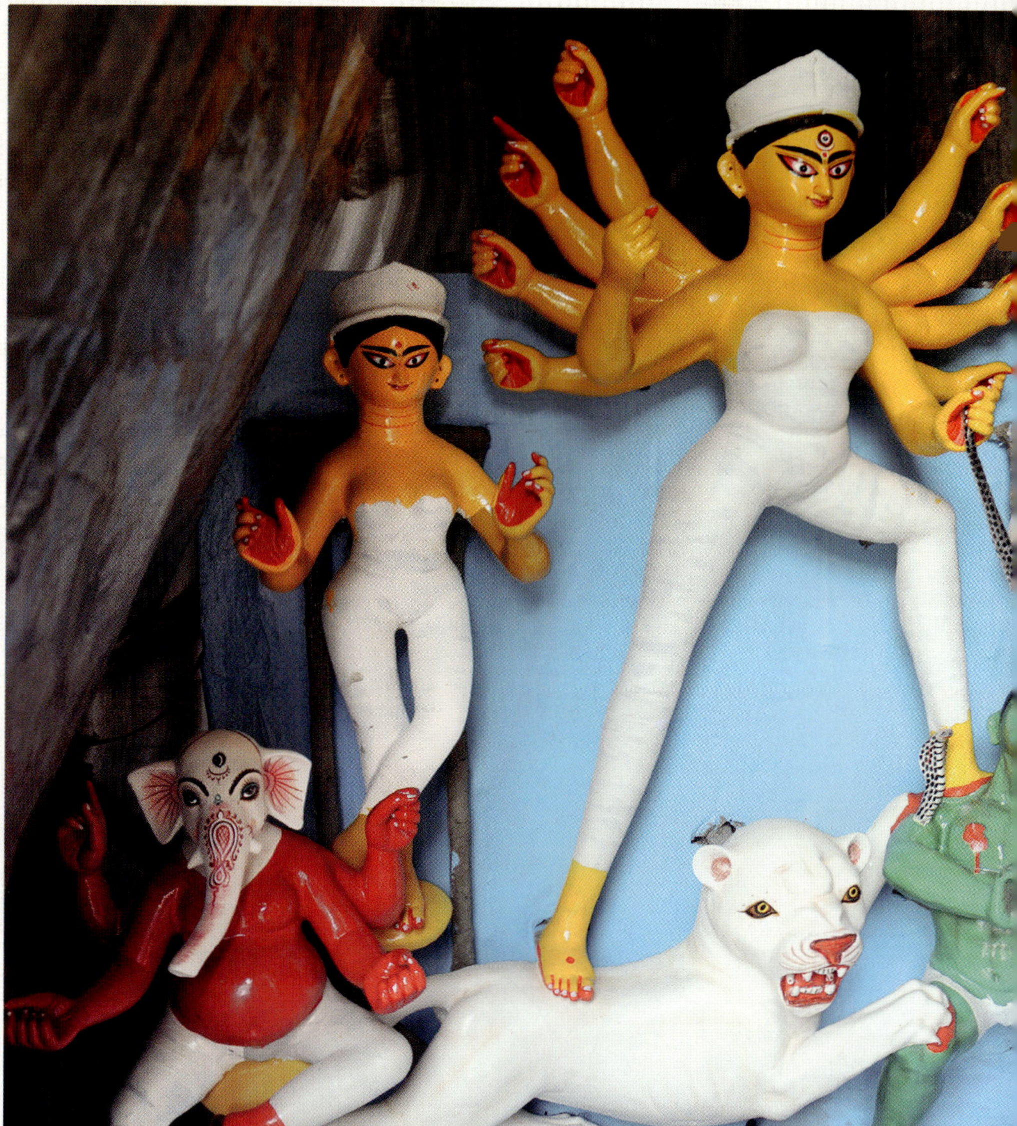

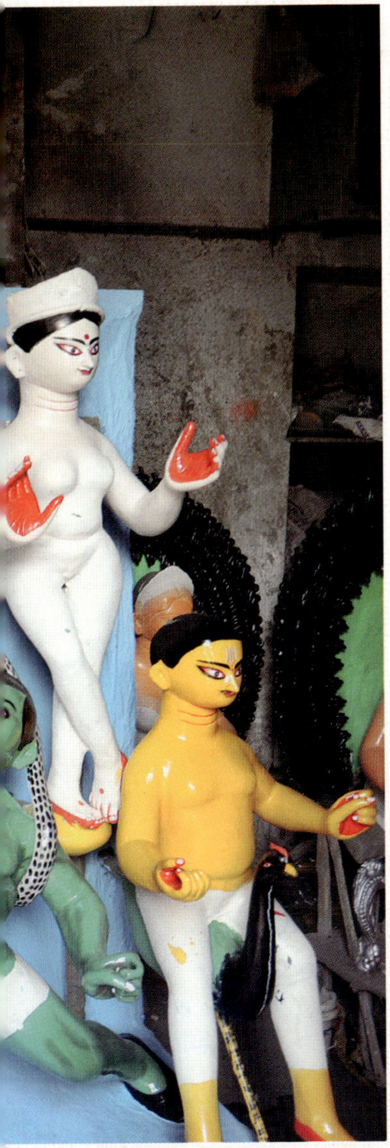

An *ekchala murti* of Godess Durga and her four children, in the making at Kumortuli

Kumortuli is a thriving colony of artisans in the north of Kolkata, fairly close to Sova Bazar metro station, between the river Hugli and the arterial road Rabindra Sarani. There is also a regular boat service to the place.

Here, for over 200 years, the icon-makers of Bengal have been making a living constructing celestial images from the Hindu pantheon. During Hindu religious festivals, these icons are sold for the annual ritual worship in private homes as well as in public spaces–all over Kolkata and beyond.

As my ancestral home happened to be near Kumortuli, I grew up watching the divine icons being made and their stalls being crafted in nearby Dompara. Some of my childhood friends lived even closer to Kumortuli. As children, we often visited the place, with the expectation that a few kindly potters would let us have bits of soft clay to play with, which seemed almost like play-dough. We made balls, coils and weird shapes with them, scoring eyes and mouth with matchsticks. Playing with our own creations was great fun.

Back in the 1950s, on my way to school as a child, I was equally fascinated by the wonderful make-believe shapes, like that of a giant swan or a fairy-tale palanquin, being constructed around an automobile by the bamboo craftsmen at nearby Dompara. What was just an unfinished bamboo frame of an ugly duckling in the morning, would turn into a splendid tissue-paper swan on my way home, as if by magic! I can still recall the sense of surprise that engulfed me.

As I grew older, other engagements, interests and experiences gradually moved me away from these haunts, but I never lost my fondness for these places. I returned to Kumortuli whenever I could, just to breathe in the soothing artistic raptness of the icon-makers in the middle of the swarming hectic city.

Amazingly, over the years, both these shanty towns have not changed much except for the ubiquitous intrusion of mobile phones. People, as ever, remain gentle, modest and friendly; working conditions still cluttered, humble and yet surprisingly productive.

This book is a tribute to the men and women who live and work in the unique and thriving colony of the artisans of Kumortuli and their co-workers at Dompara who create equally fascinating structures of temporary divine abodes for the gods.

Like the cave paintings of Ajanta near Mumbai and the sculptures of the Sun Temple at Konark, Odisha, these unique and enduring methods of making icons and their stalls at Kumortuli and Dompara, are also parts of our broader artistic and cultural heritage. Since these works, unlike stone sculpture or mural painting, are essentially ephemeral, they are in even greater need of documentation, conservation and special protection.

With this motivation, I have attempted to convey the sight, sound and smell of these little-known creative domains in Kolkata through words and photographs, with relevant historical and cultural information, but without much use of specialist

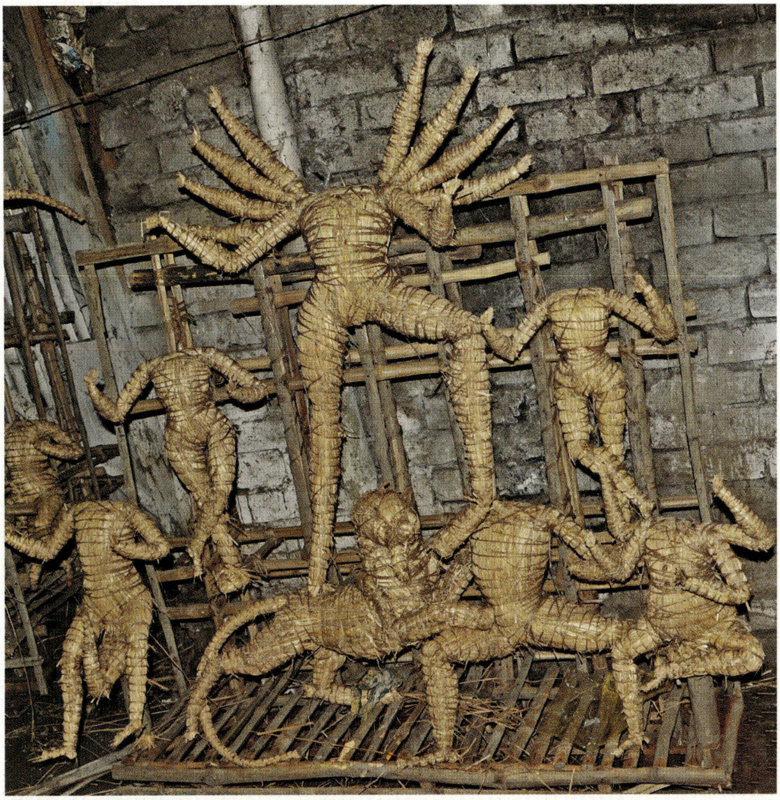

terminology. I have often used the Sanskrit word *murti* for clay images, because the word invokes divine reality in many shapes and forms, be it an icon or a rock. The word is now familiar among the Western academics of Hinduism.

Throughout the book, I have consciously used both nomenclatures, Calcutta and Kolkata, for chronological reasons. Most references to pre-1990 period retain the old spelling of Calcutta to capture the historic flavour of the place.

I hope this book will be a useful resource and an absorbing guide for readers across cultures.

The straw structure which defines the basic form of the icon

*Together the fragments of celestial
and ordinary life construct a
fantastic display of divine tableaux.*

Kumortuli

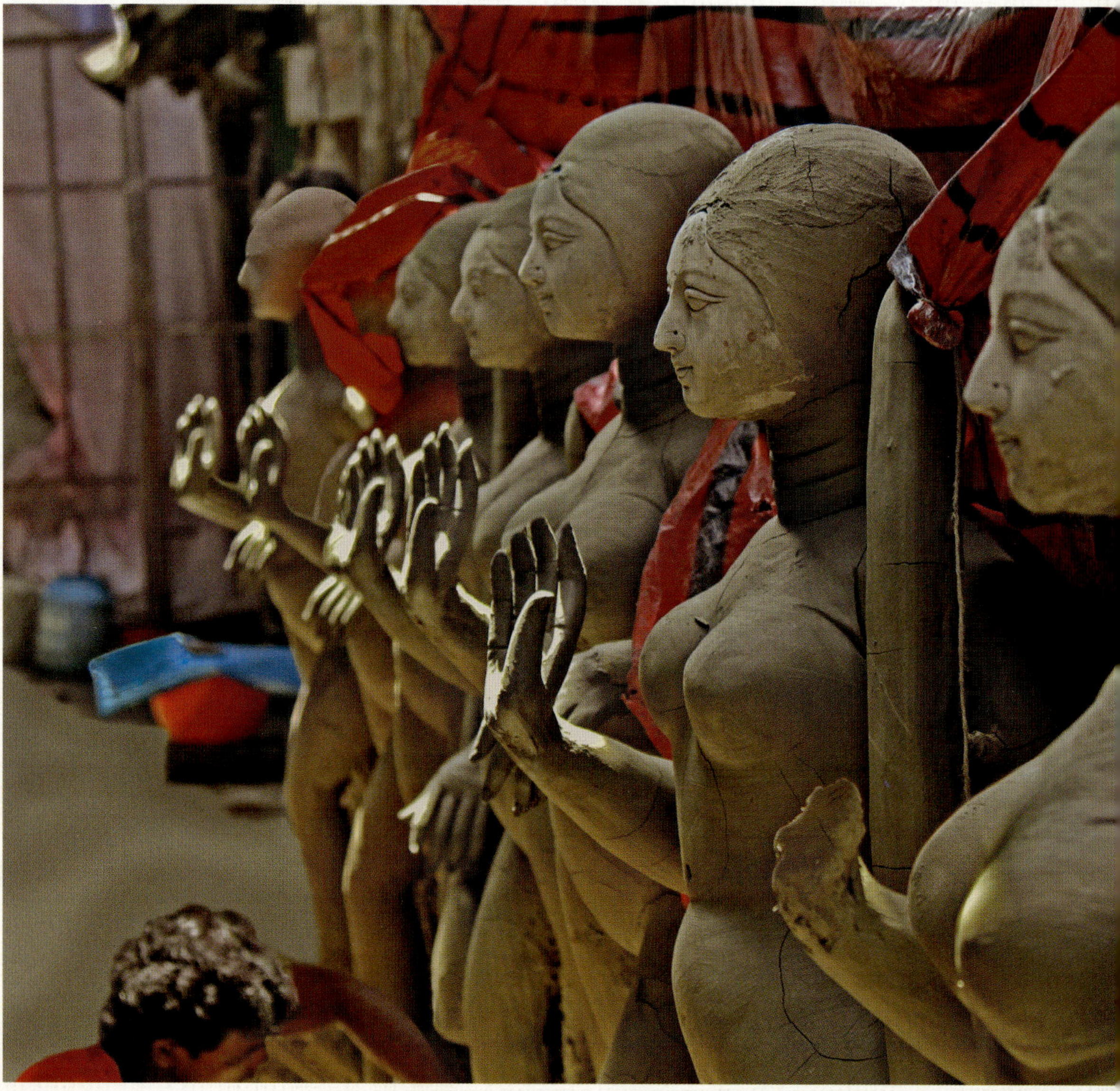

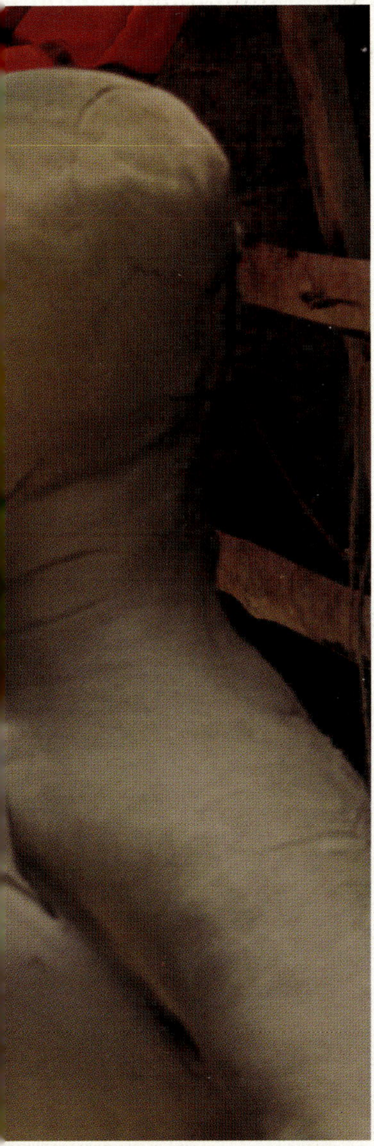

Within 5 acres of Kumortuli's narrow sinewy pathways, further cramped by heaps of raw material and half-finished icons strewn around at various stages of construction, you can watch the entire process of shaping divine images. As you walk down, you will see clay body parts like arms, feet and fingers drying in the sun, rows of faces freshly prised out of a mould being painted with a white undercoat, basic straw structure of a full figure being mounted on a bamboo stand with hammer and nails. The whole place feels surreal with bits of recognisable human and animal forms among the artisans and their helpers, while wives, children and pets mill around. Some might be clutching spatulas, brushes, scissors, bits of string and shiny

both: Life goes on... amidst the half-finished icons and various clay body parts drying in the sun along the roadside

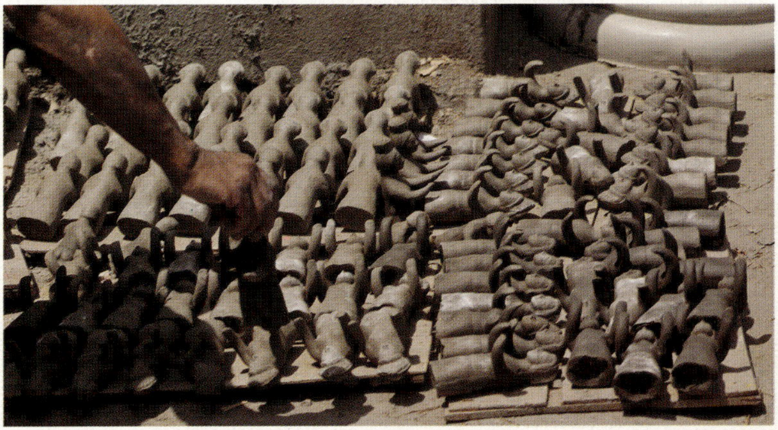

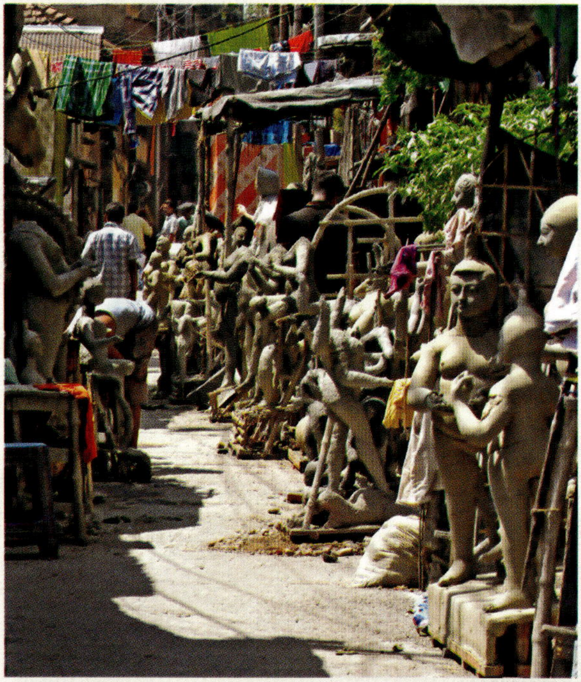

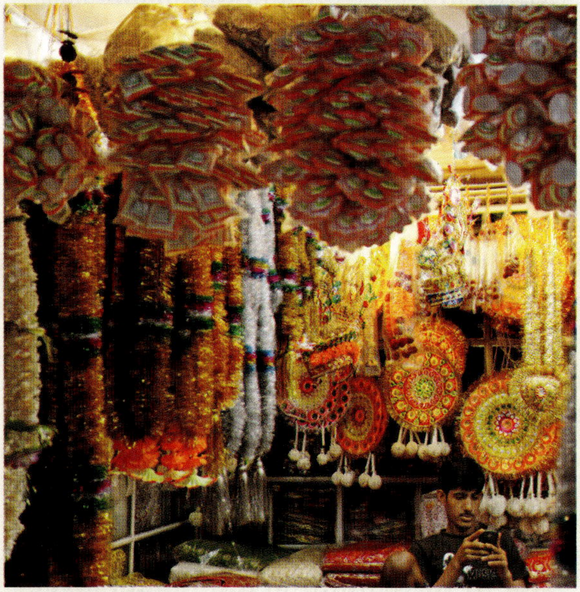

materials, bunches of black nylon hair and its likes to be put on the clay models. Surprisingly, amidst Kumortuli's palpable impoverishment, everyday activities such as cooking, washing and drying clothes, tending babies continue alongside the absorbing creation of the celestial world.

Together the fragments of celestial and ordinary life construct a fantastic display of divine tableaux. Mundane materials like clay, bamboo, strings and straw form the core structure and the pith of *shola* reeds, tinsel, coloured paper and sequins used for embellishment, create amazing exhibits. Often children can be spotted making gorgeous jewellery and ornaments for the deities by cutting out intricate patterns from coloured tin foil and flattened shola pith sheets with rudimentary tools such as pencils, penknives and razorblades. Women can be seen straightening the straws and smearing skeins of jute with liquid made from soft chalk and clay or combing strands of false hair, while men on ladders repair hairline cracks on the framed forms.

All through the year, the place is a hive of gentle activity as the icon-makers slowly create religious images, busts and statuettes of iconic people like Mahatma Gandhi, Mother Teresa, Rabindranath Tagore and Swami Vivekananda. However, the place becomes frenetic from April-

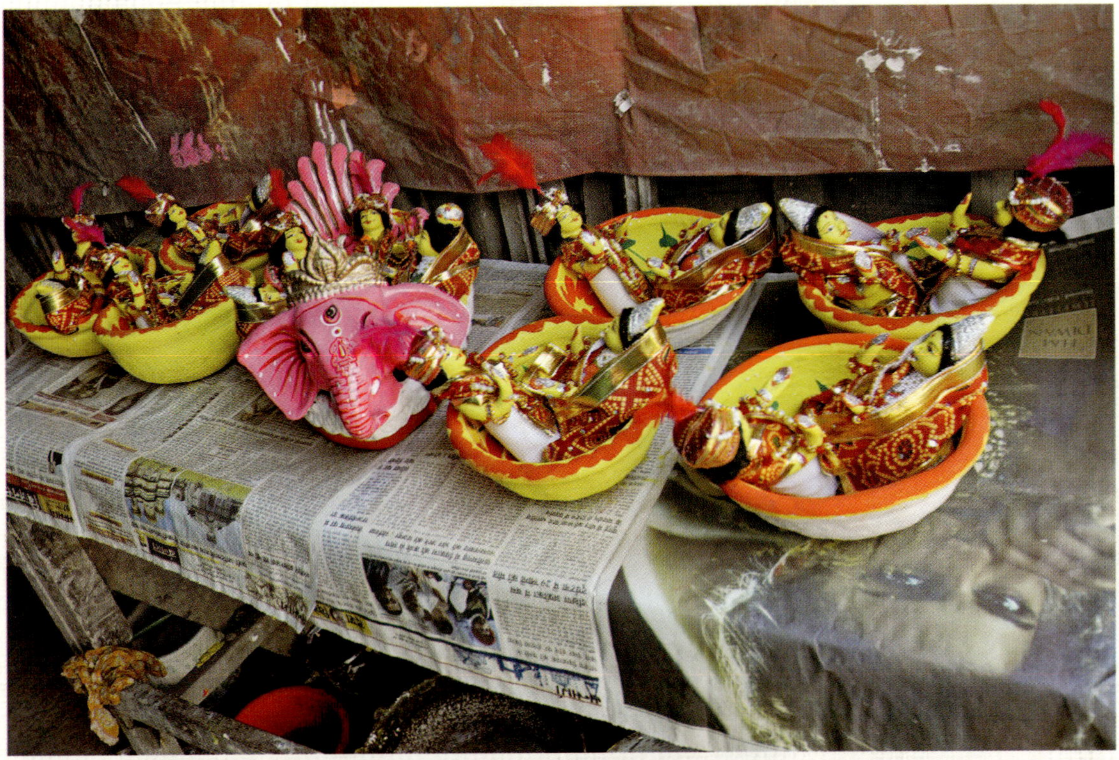

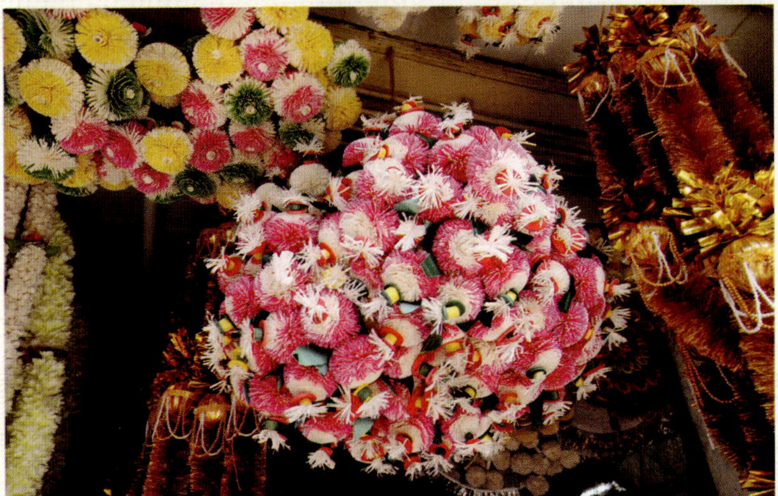

above, left and facing page (below): Colourful non-religious toys and decorative items on display for sale

facing page: (above) Icons left outside the workshops to dry in the sun after the first layering of clay

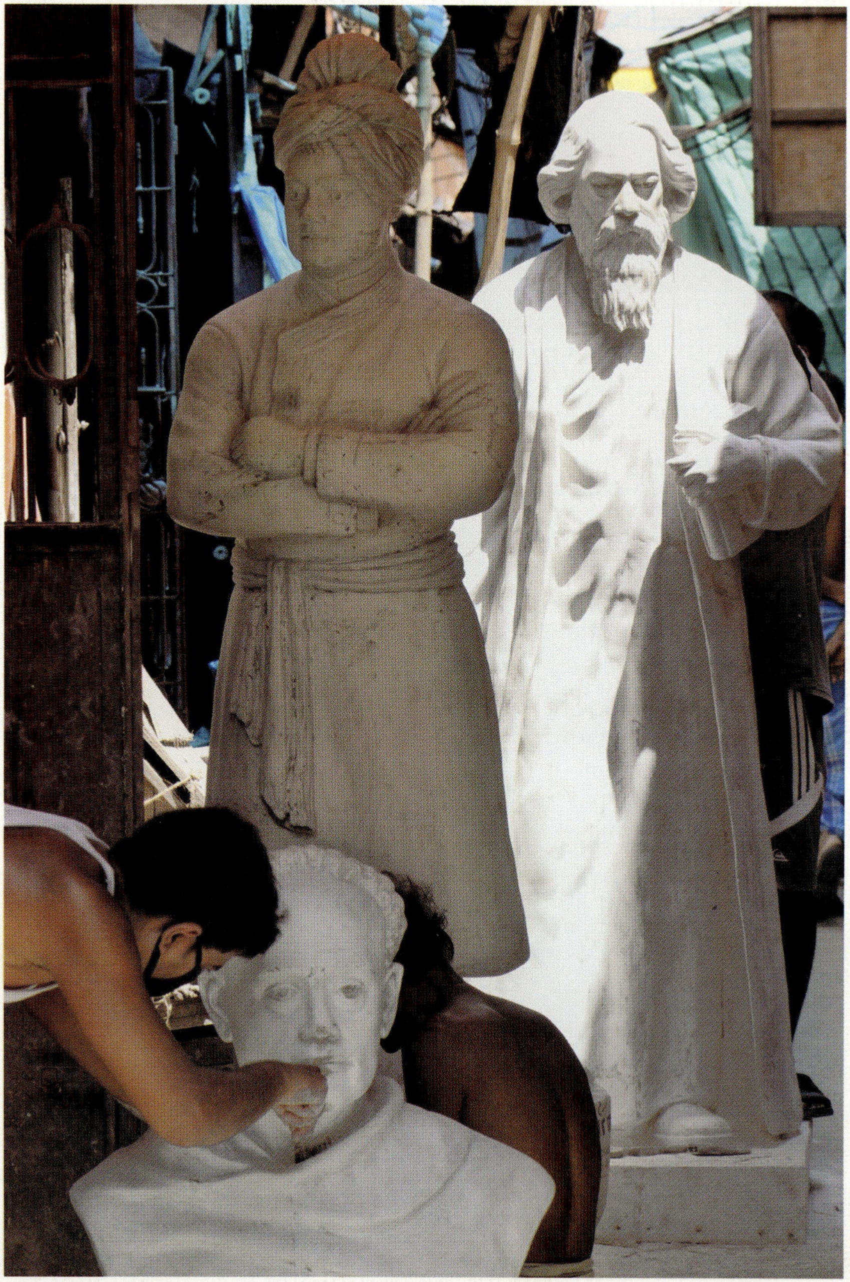

A *kumor* making statues of Tagore, Vivekananda and Vidyasagar.

May to September-October supplying icons for the major Bengali festivals, Durga Puja and Kali Puja. Since the 1980s they have also been delivering Durga *murtis* to a global clientele in Africa, America, Australia and Europe—wherever there are Bengali Hindu expatriate communities.

The icon-making fraternity of Kumortuli has also initiated and supported a whole raft of specialist craftsmen and craftswomen who not only aid their work, but are integral to the whole operation. For example, the artists who ritually paint the divine eyes; the drapers who dress the gods and goddesses; the craftsmen of shola pith, sequins and coloured paper and the artisans from nearby Dompara who design the decorative bamboo structures (known as pandals) to accommodate the deity during the annual celebration of Durga Puja.

A web of trade and commerce too, has evolved around this industry of icon-making. For example, the suppliers of the bluish clay soil to complement the greyish local silt for modelling the deities, the providers of paddy straw for the construction of the celestial body shapes and the boatmen who transport these over the river Hugli,

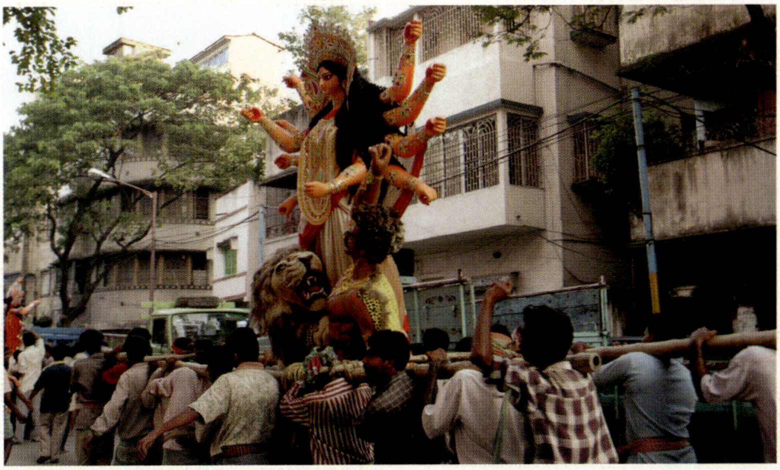

A common sight on Kolkata streets just before Durga Puja

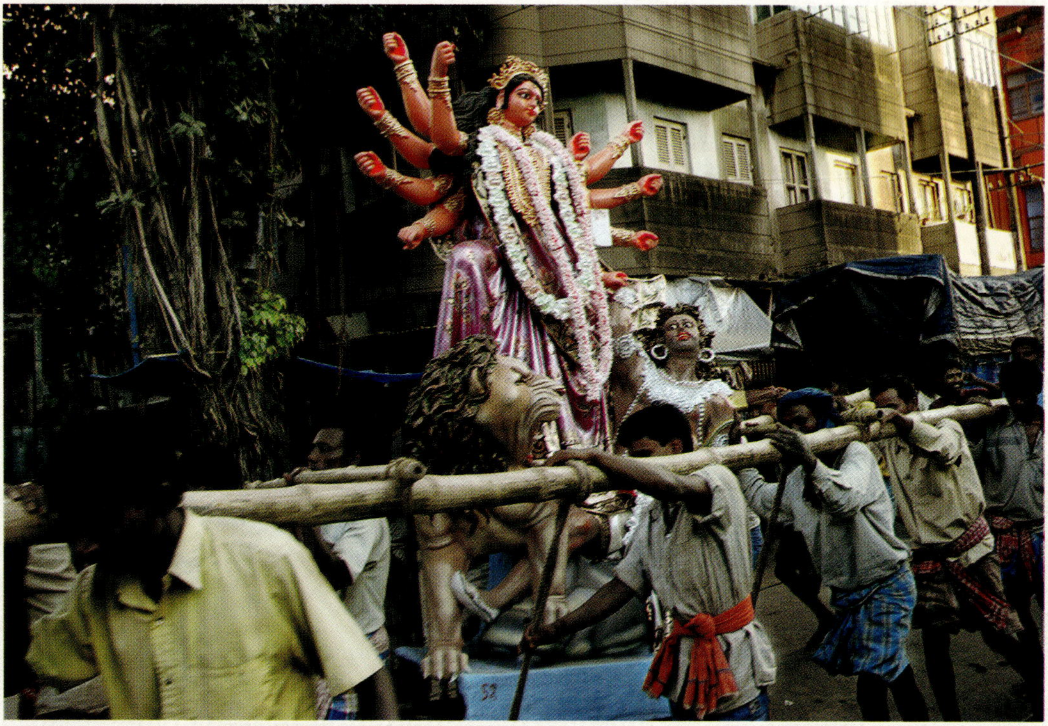

which runs behind the neighbourhood. Then there are the bamboo stretcher bearers who move the icons out from the workshops to the main street and the lorry drivers who finally deliver the large creations, 10-20 feet high, to the venues.

The exact details of how this special colony of craftsmen settled here are difficult to determine but this much is known, originally the area was a dense jungle infested with bandits, pilgrims and wild animals. Then, slowly a community grew around the ancient temple of Chitteswari. From 1760 onwards, the lure of better financial prospects through association with the traders of the East India Company, drew aspiring Bengali residents to settle in the surrounding areas. For example, the legendary landlord, Gobindaram Mitra; the tax collector for the East India Company,

An icon of Goddess Durga on its way to the pandal

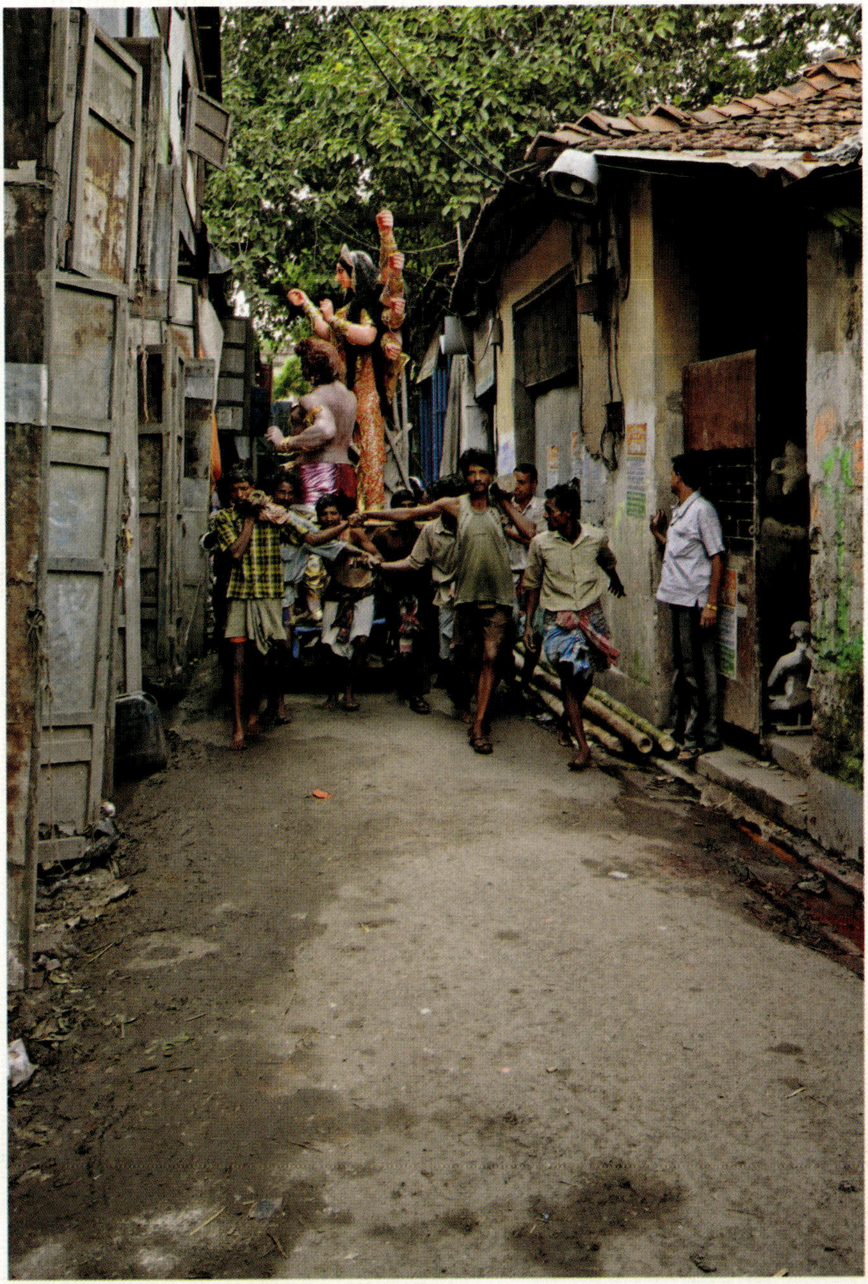

Stretcher bearers delivering finished icons, deftly negotiating narrow alleyways

Banamali Sarker; the Marwari merchants like the famously bearded Umichand; the moneylender to the Company, Hujurimal, and others were all living in and operating from this area. A visit to the nearby imposing bone-grey Palladian mansion built around 1830s, stuffed with an eclectic assortment of European art and artefacts, could give an inkling into the lifestyle of these men who made their fortunes cooperating with the first batch of the British East India Company merchants.

After the defeat of Siraj ud-daulah, the ruler of Bengal, at the battle of Polashi (Plassey) in 1757, this community developed further as an urban settlement for the locals. Large brick-built family houses with flat roofs and hanging verandas, street markets, temples, mosques and warehouses were built for them. This nouveau riche generation also developed a taste for foreign objects and acquired a great deal of European art and artefacts to adorn their grand houses and gardens, thus accidentally introducing Western art and sculpture to India.

The artisans of Kumortuli too seem to have been influenced by classical sculptures from the Greek pantheon. Thus, the images of the male deities look strikingly Apollonian and naturalistic though the female figures remain traditionally stylised and curved.

The area around Kumortuli gradually came to be known as Black Town in contrast to the White Town where the white settlers resided in spacious houses among clean, wide, tree-lined streets. As you travel through Kolkata, the relics of the divided city are still visible.

Soon groups of weavers, tailors, coppersmiths, tanners, oil pressers, metal workers, potters and many more arrived in this quarter, to serve the indigenous community with everyday objects, groceries, etc. As they began to form their separate living clusters denoted by their profession, they acquired Bengali names for their areas, reflecting their trade. Thus, Darjipara became the settlement of the tailors (*darji*), Muchipara the settlement of the tanners (*muchi*), Kolutola housed the oil pressers (*kolu*) and Kumortuli became the neighbourhood of the *kumors* – the potters of utility earthenware, clay dolls and icons.

The 1876 Census, under the guidance of civil servant and later historian Sir William W. Hunter, first records the potters under 'occupation of lower order' in Calcutta. But we know they were present in the area long before. The Flemish journeyman artist Balthazar Solvyns (1760-1824) recorded the icons-makers with other local workers like the weavers and sweepers around 1790.

Kumors are supposed to have a divine ancestor, Brahma—the creator of the world.

The Kumors

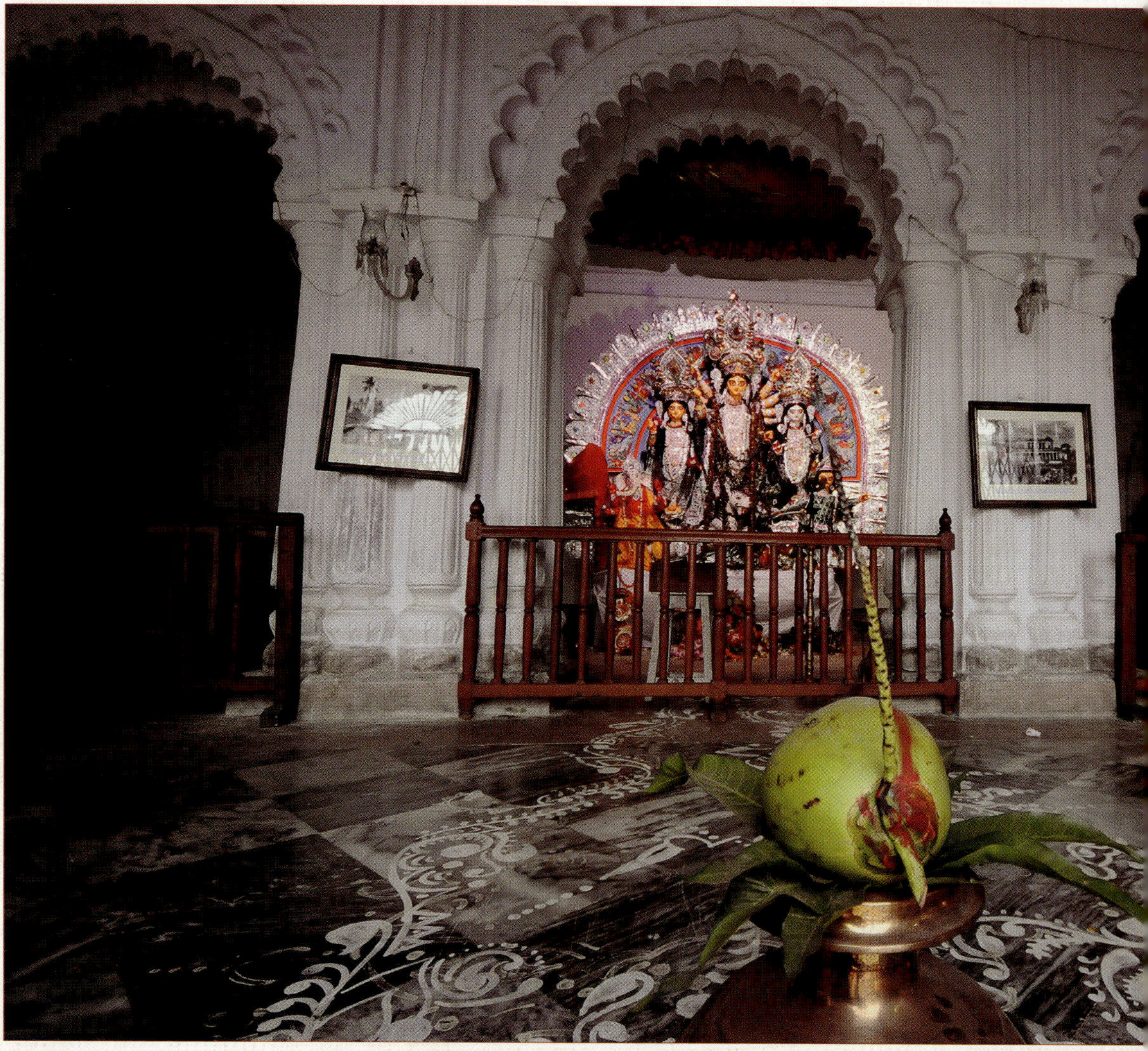

Kumor is a corrupt colloquial form of the Sanskrit word *kumbhokar* meaning the maker of clay water pitchers, and *tuli* implies locality. Hence, the compound Bengali term 'kumortuli' means potters' quarter—by extension, the home of the icon-makers.

Kumors are supposed to have a divine ancestor, Brahma—the creator of the world. According to Hindu scriptures, the Puranas, they produced the very first pot (or *ghot* as said in Bengali and pronounced similar to 'pot') to hold the ambrosia gleaned from the ocean churned by the gods and the demons. The myth of churning of the ocean (*Samudramanthan*) narrated in a later section, is well-known throughout India.

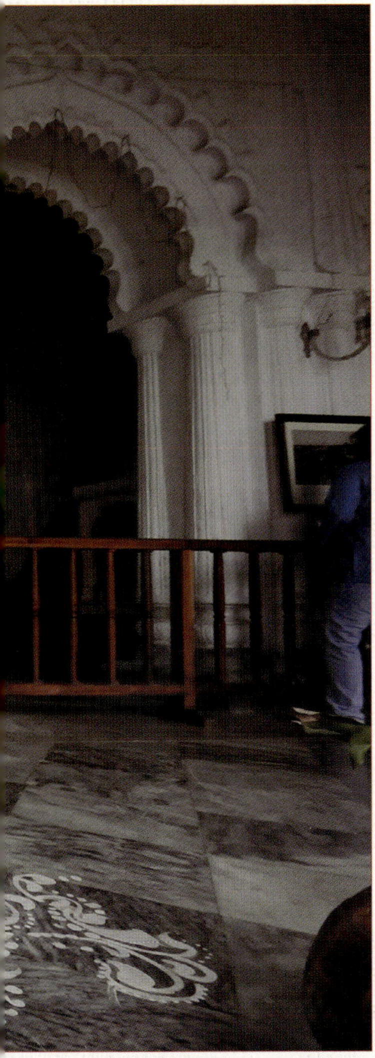

The *thakurdalan* of one of the great ancestral houses of Kolkata with a *ghot* in the foreground

Pots or *ghots* have a special place in Hinduism. To a Hindu, a *ghot* is not just an ordinary vessel, it is a sacred receptacle of great spiritual and mystical significance. Devotees invoke a deity through chants and prayer to enter the sacrosanct pot and accept their adoration. Long before icon worship became the norm, Hindus venerated sanctified clay ghots provided by the *kumors*. Even now, on special occasions, *ghots* are widely worshipped at homes all over India. Often, a decorated *ghot* with a vermillion-smeared coconut draped in a hibiscus or marigold garland on top, can be seen at the entrance of a house or a shrine on ceremonial days, symbolising the holiness of the premises.

Raja Krishna Chandra Ray (1710-82) of Nabadwip, a patron of the arts, is said to have encouraged the *kumors* from neighbouring villages of Bansbedey, Shantipur and Ghurni to travel to Calcutta—then a fast growing city—and to offer their wares and craftsmanship to the affluent Bengalis living in Black Town. Today's potters are their descendants.

However, the artisans of Kumortuli are not potters in the usual sense, though they occasionally make pitchers and pots. They are in fact, clay icon-modellers or *murti*-makers.

In the past, the icon-makers were commissioned to go and reside in the private homes of the rich and famous Bengalis, for about a month or longer, to build the icon in-situ. These houses contained a dedicated terraced space for worship known as *thakurdalan*–hall of the deity. The family provided food and temporary lodging to these people throughout and remuneration with tips on completion. Only few historic houses in Kolkata and its suburbs still continue with the tradition. *Utsav*, a Bengali movie made in 2000 by the Late Rituparno Ghosh, sensitively documents the entire process.

Some icon-makers these days have taken up other works as clerks, artists and sculptors, but at the time of Durga Puja around September-October they all lend a hand to meet the huge demand of orders for the divine images. Among these artisans some have even attended art colleges to enrich themselves and give new directions to the traditional iconography. Some have large studio spaces elsewhere in the city. But the overall ambience of Kumortuli—its smell of wet clay and straw and potters occupied

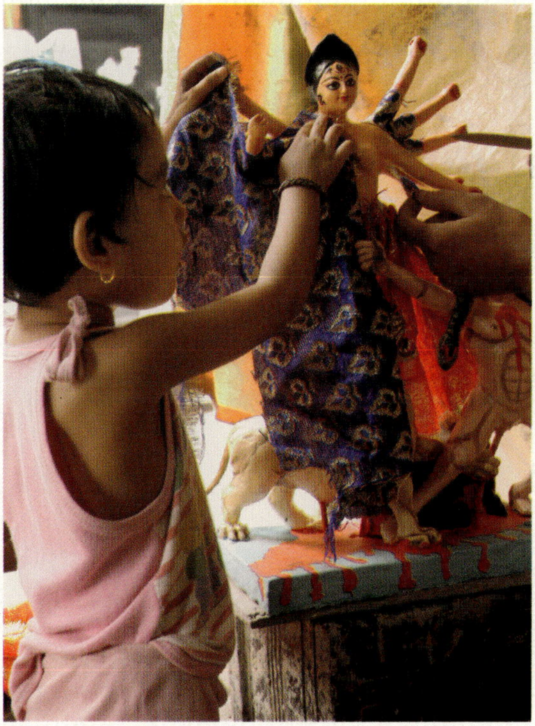

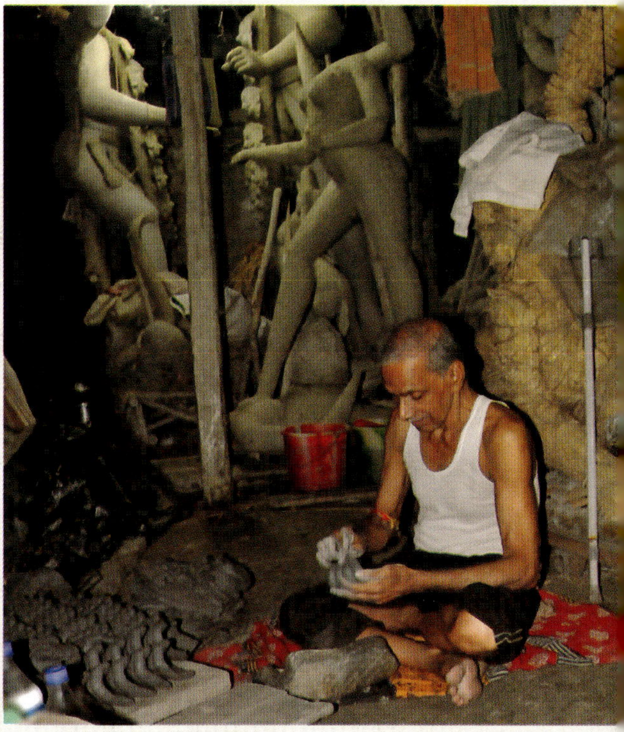

in creative concentration against the background of rows of half-finished icons with raw materials scattered around—remains unchanged. One can usually wander freely to watch the *murti*-makers in action except for the busiest time when a special permission may be required.

both: A budding *kumor* in training, while the veteran one carries on as usual

In recent years, the concept of resettling this community to a purpose-built colony has been discussed but nothing has been decided yet. I asked one octogenarian potter about the future of icon-making in our fast-changing century. He reassured me, 'As long as the Bengalis live, Durga Puja will go on, so there is no immediate threat to our profession. We have survived famine, partition and riots and for survival we have adapted to new ideas and materials. We will survive.'

Indeed, the icon-makers have already reinvented their art using a different man-made material. Since the 1980s they have been making icons from a polystyrene block known in India as thermocole. Unlike the pith of *shola* used in some image crafts, these blocks are less fragile, lighter and less costly for mailing abroad. Thermocole now provides divine icons to about 90 countries in Europe, America, Australia and Russia to keep up with the ever-growing demands from overseas Bengali communities. Many dedicated agents in Kolkata now deal with foreign sales and transportation of polystyrene icons to most places in the world. There are many small and inconspicuous studios and shop-fronts around Kumortuli, manufacturing polystyrene Durga *murtis* fully painted,

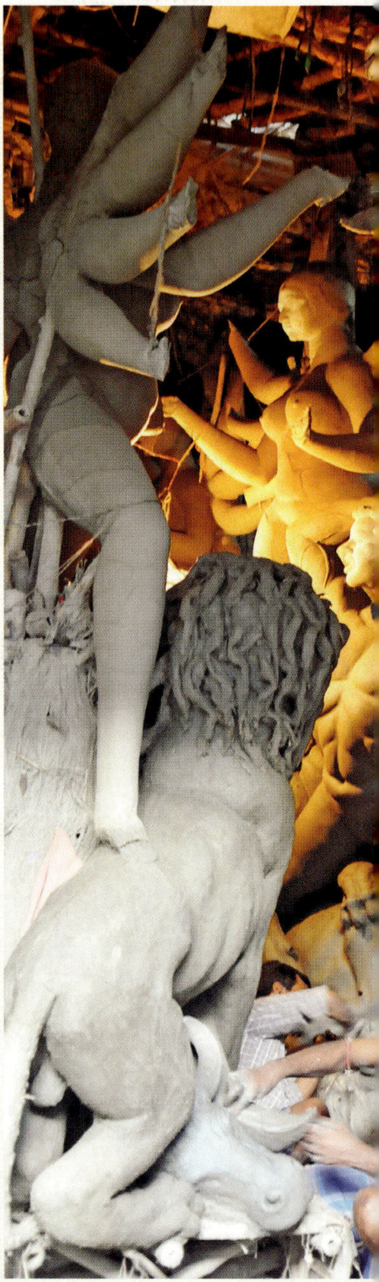

both right and below: *Kumors* at work in their studios

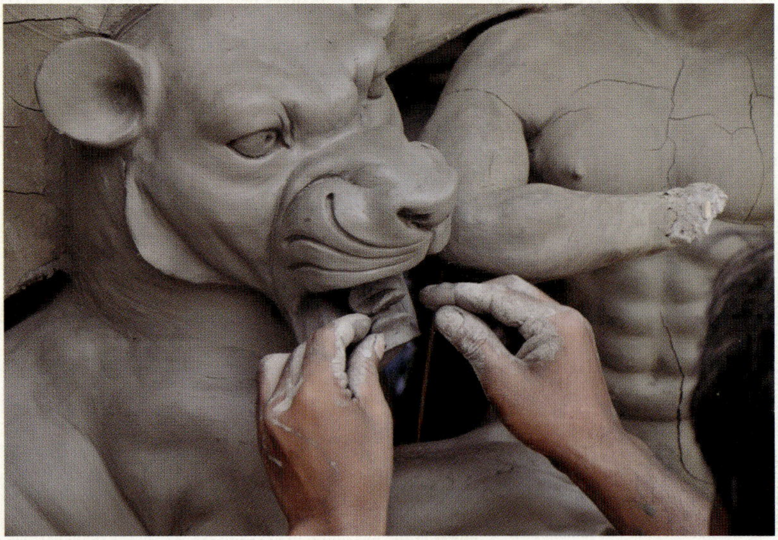

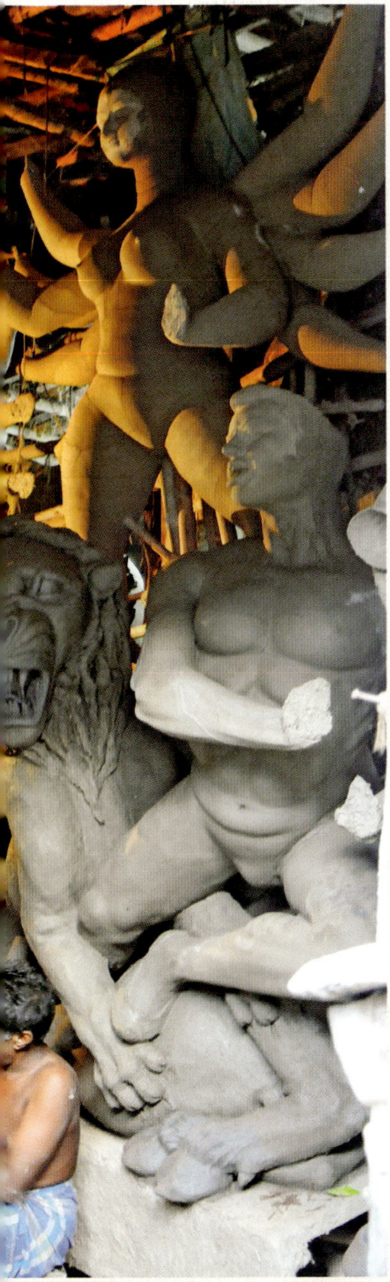

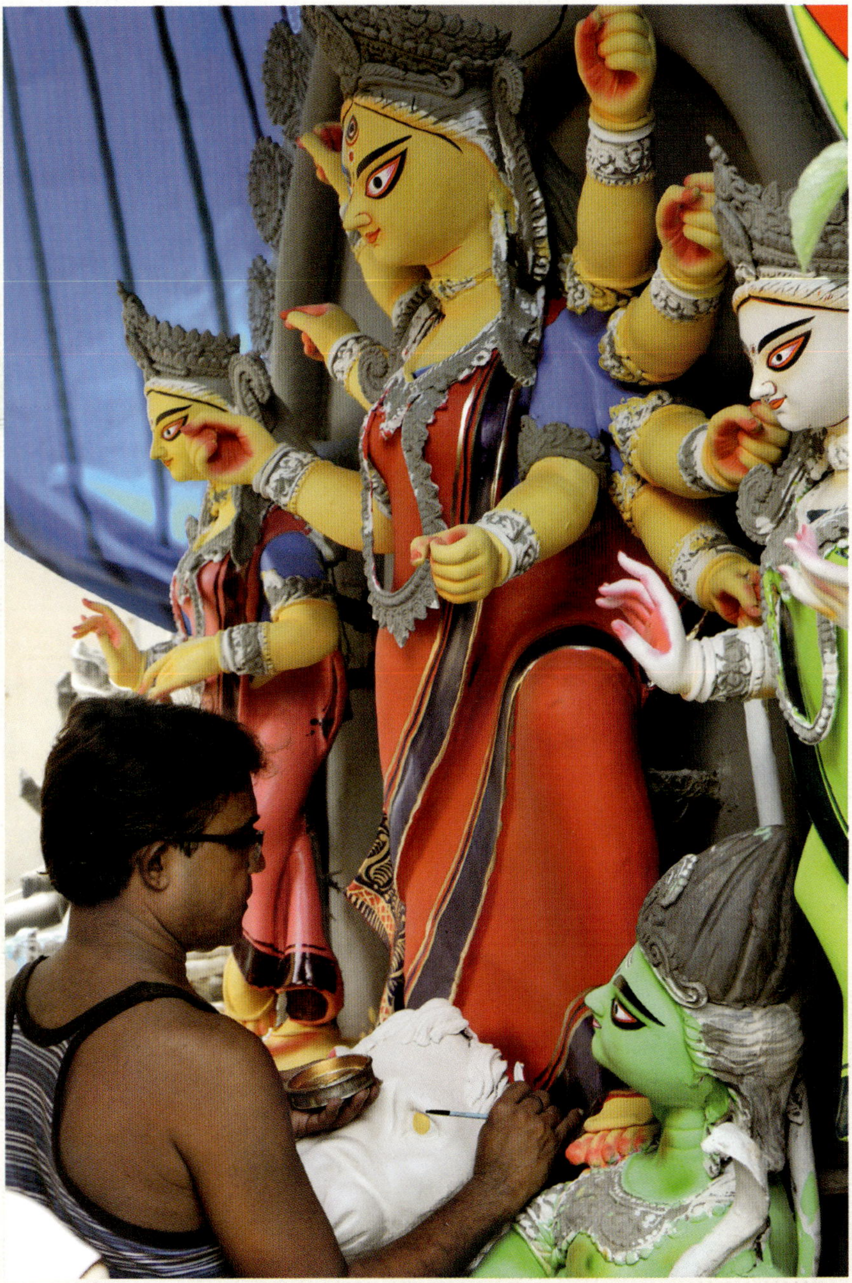

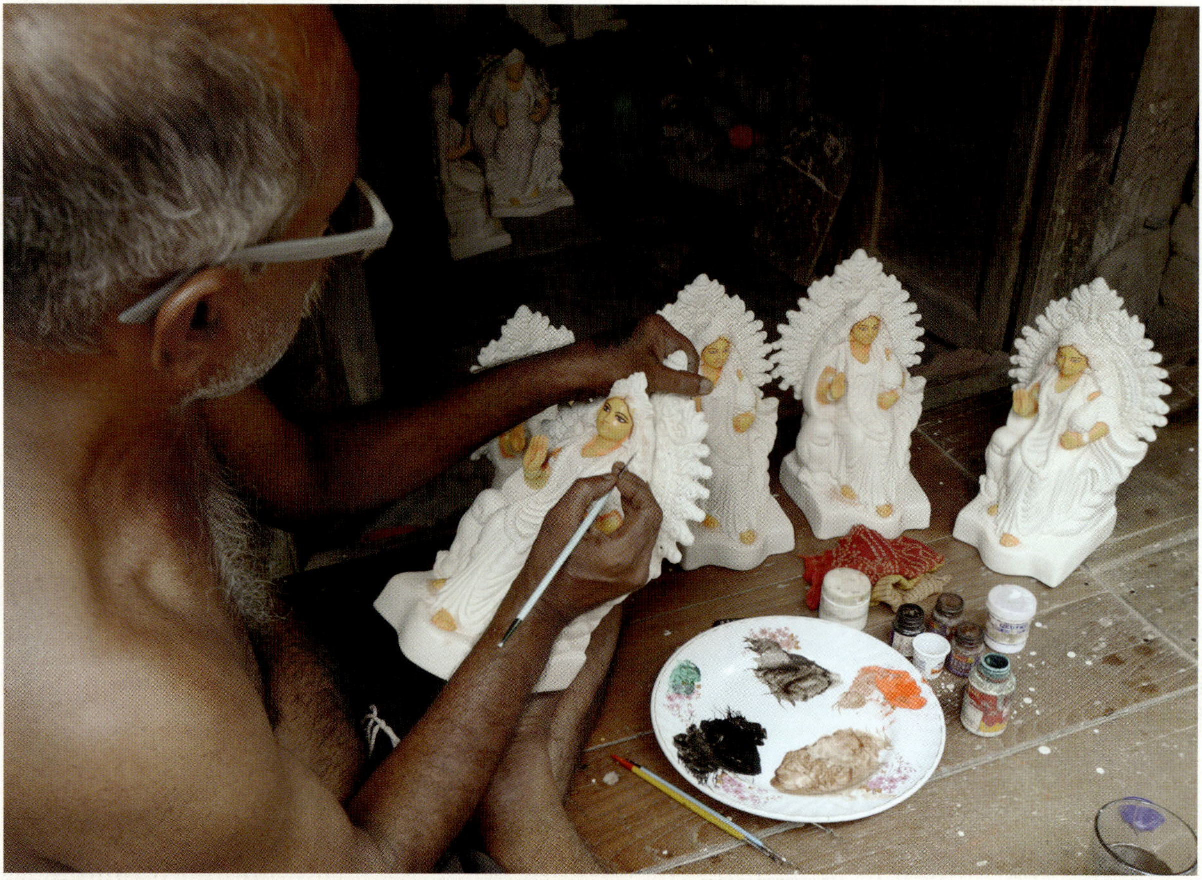

draped and embellished, ready to be sent overseas. To maintain the individuality of godly features, the icon-makers do not largely use uniform moulds but skilfully carve out features from solid slabs of polystyrene with various sculpting tools. Every *murti* is handmade.

Some eminent icon-makers even dictate the style of the surrounding décor, lighting and the choice of music for the service, often preferring subdued light to flashing strobes, and devotional songs to Hindi film music.

A *kumor* painting the face of an icon

Among the most celebrated icon-makers are Mohon Banshi Rudra and his three sons, Rakhal Pal, Ganesh Pal, Kartik Pal, and Aloke Sen. There are also about thirty women potters—Minati Pal, Champa Rani Pal and Soma Pal to name a few. There are also many child potters helping all around. Kumortuli is the only thriving artisans' colony in Kolkata. Some 4000 potters work here and they deliver over 10,000 Durga *murtis* each year.

Besides Durga icons, throughout the year they make other images of Hindu divinity such as Kali, Lakshmi, Jagatdhatri, Annapurna, Saraswati, Ganesh, Kartik and other minor deities widely worshipped in Bengal.

There are many varieties of clay,
but for making the icons two
particular kinds are used.

The Process of Icon-making

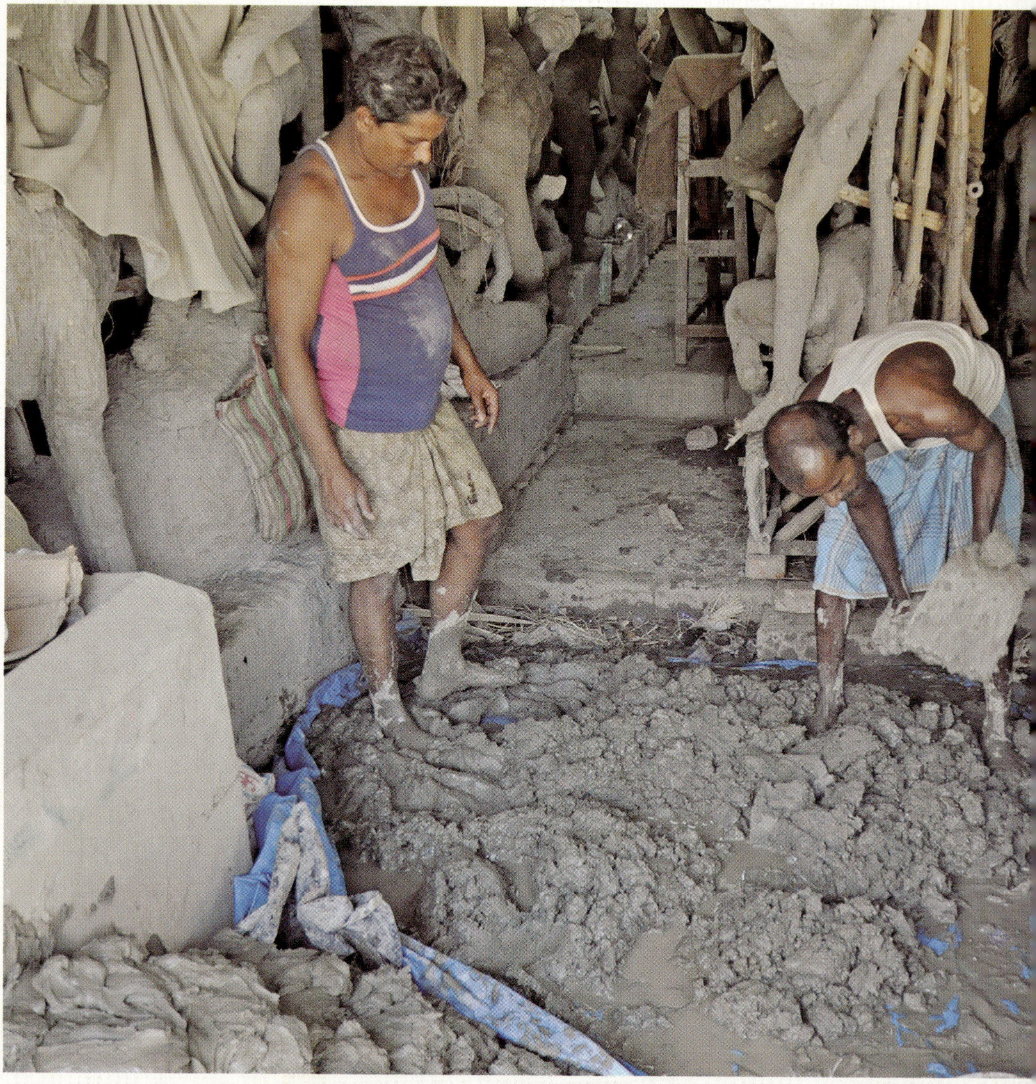

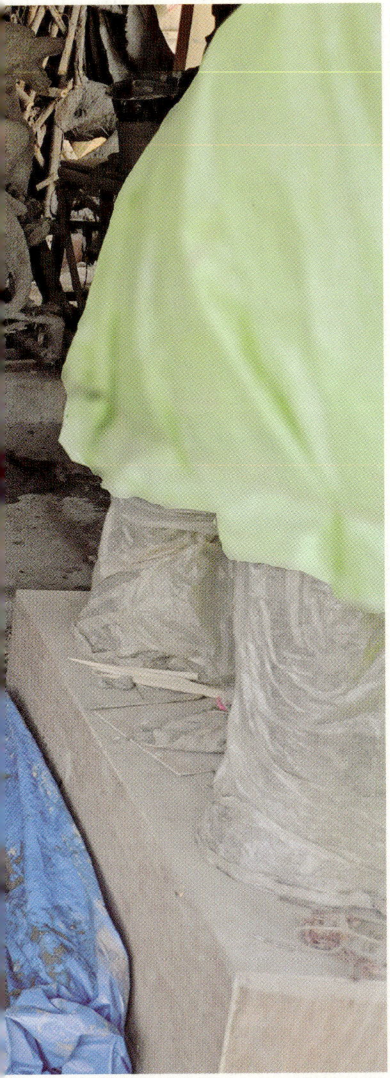

The rudimentary ingredients of icon-making are paddy straw, string, jute and clay. Straw comes by boat from the wetland mangroves of the Sunderbans—a UNESCO world heritage site.

left: Mixing the two varieties of clay

below: *Entelmati* (clay soil) being brought in by waterway

There are many varieties of clay, but for making the icons two particular kinds are used. The local soft clay (*belemati*) is plentiful in the river Hugli but the hard clay

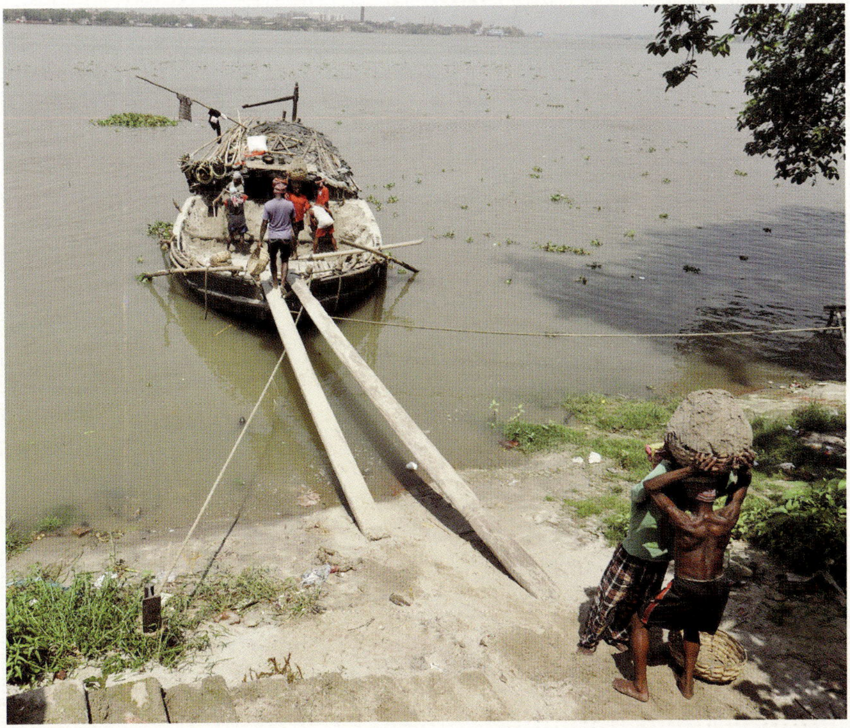

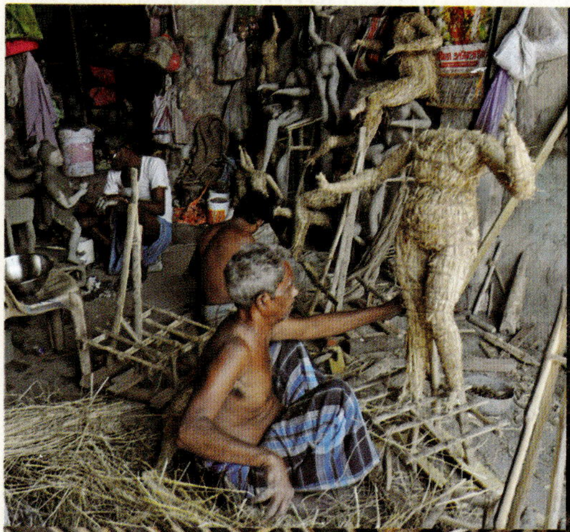

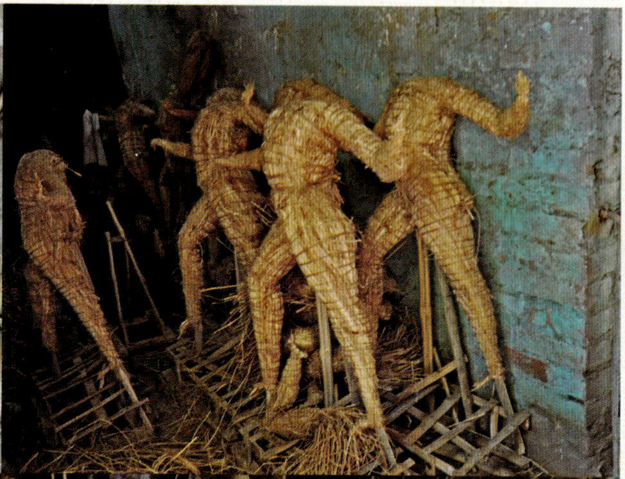

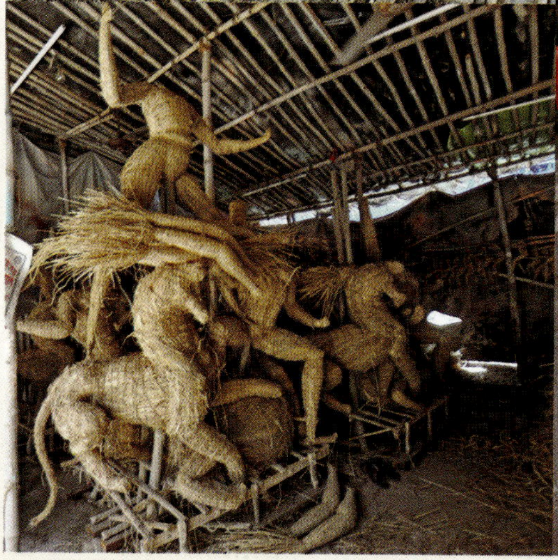

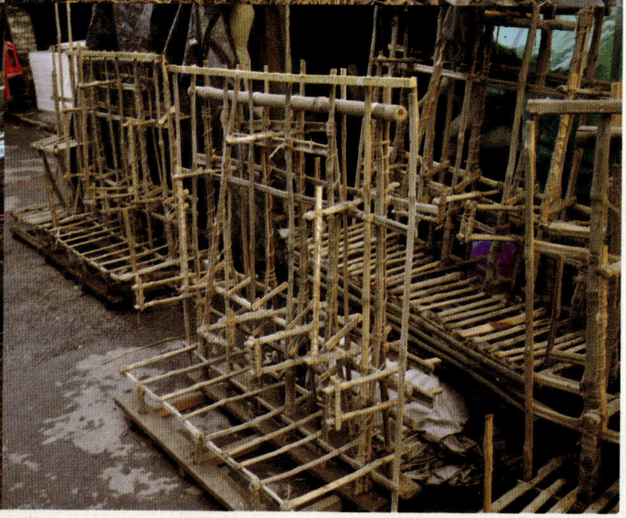

(*entelmati*) comes by boat mainly from the Diamond Harbour area in the southern suburb of Kolkata where the river meets the Bay of Bengal. The soft clay is lighter in colour than the hard kind. A half and half mixture of these two kinds is refined by sieve and sundried a little to give the required strength and stability so that a good final finish can be achieved. In some cases, finely shredded jute and straw are added to reduce the onset of cracks.

above left and right, and below left: Making the basic body structure of the icons with straw and string

These days, primary construction begins around April-May to meet the ever-growing demand. Once the bamboo and wood structure frame is constructed or rescued from immersed ones using industrial cranes, the basic body shape of the icon is formed using bunches of pliable straw tied with string in cylindrical shapes. After the body framework is made, it is daubed with clay mixture. While that is left to dry, the face and the fingers are cast using moulds and gradually attached to the body structure. Cracks developing on the drying icons at this stage are immediately patched with pieces of rag and layers of clay wash. Usually two layers of clay washes are applied, followed by a quick jet of blowtorch for rapid drying. When the clay body is finally dried with no cracks, the first undercoat of white paint is applied. It takes at least four to six weeks to reach this stage, depending on the arrival of monsoon. Then the second coat of yellow is applied,

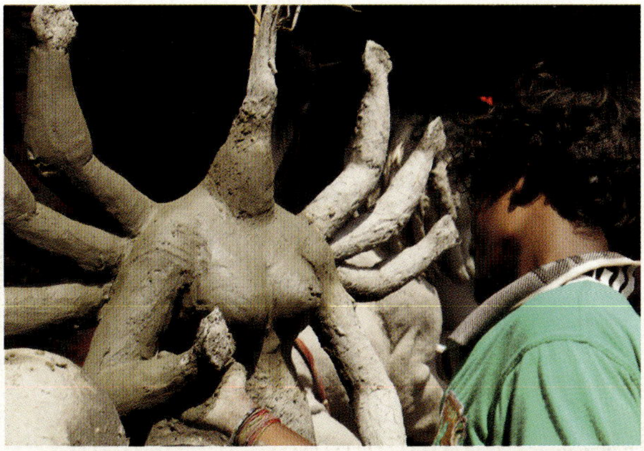

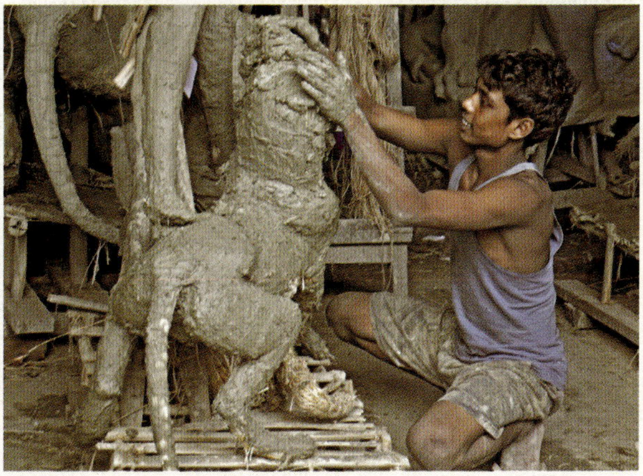

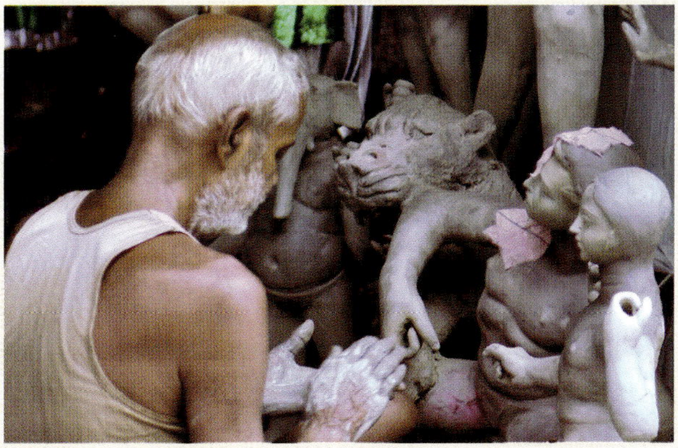

right above and below: Applying the first layer of clay

left: An experienced hand repairing cracks

facing page below right: *Kathamo*—pedestal for the icon

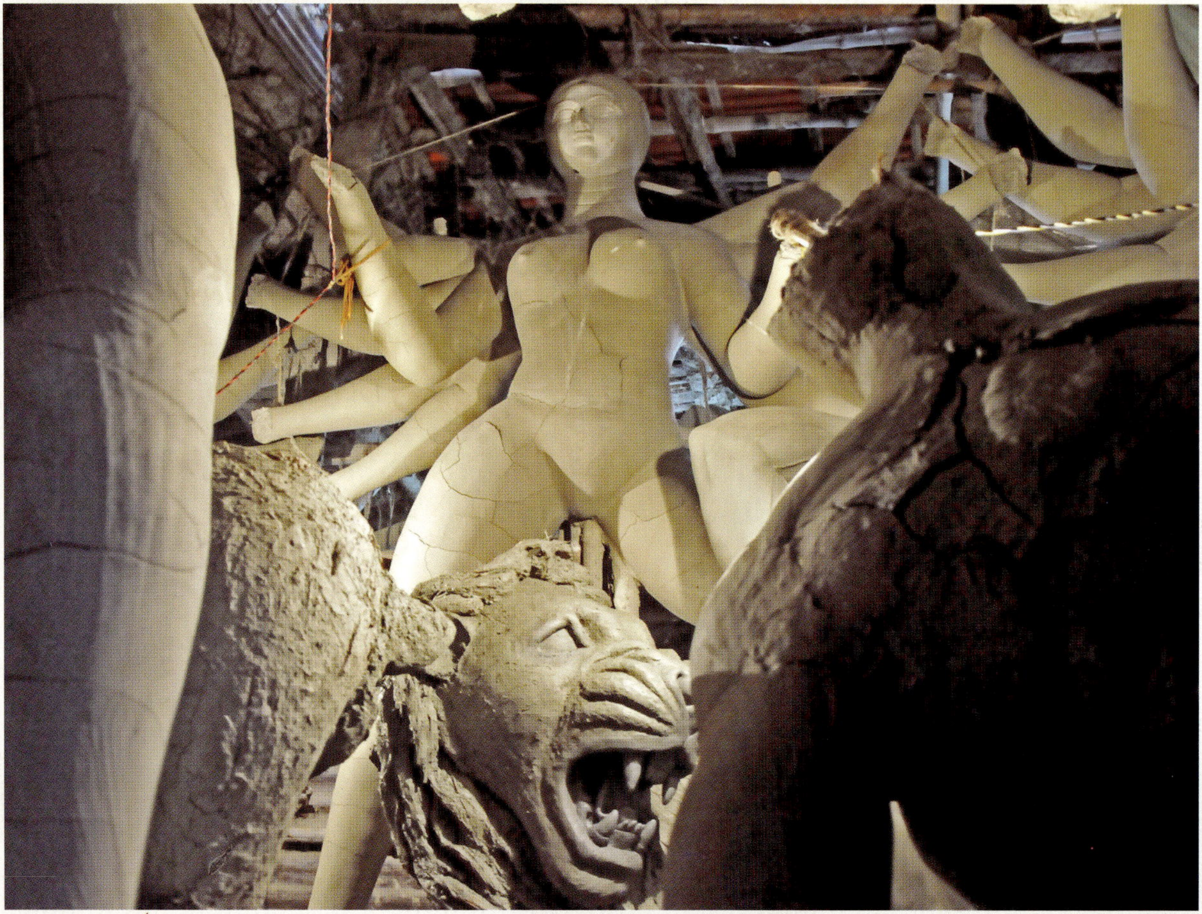

above and facing page: More cracks appearing as the first layer of clay dries

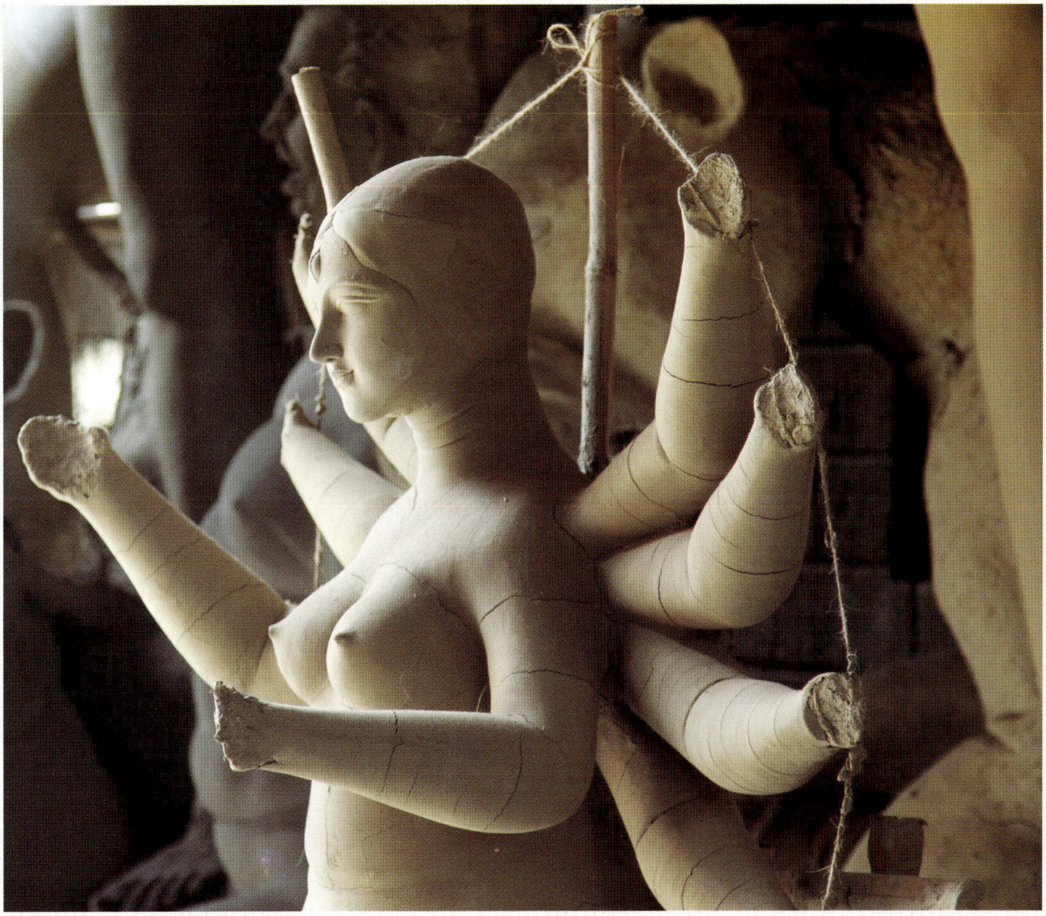

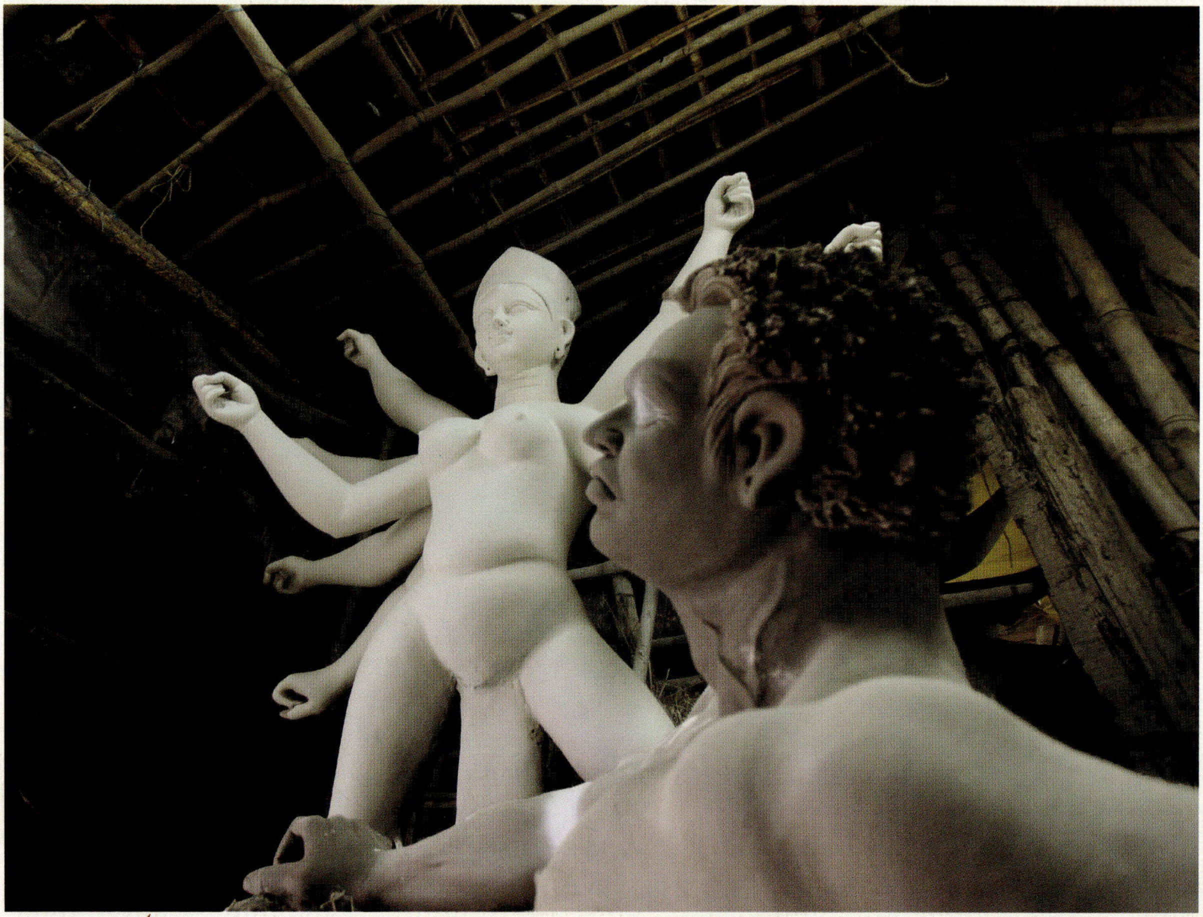

above and facing page: Smoothly finished icons with a second coating of clay

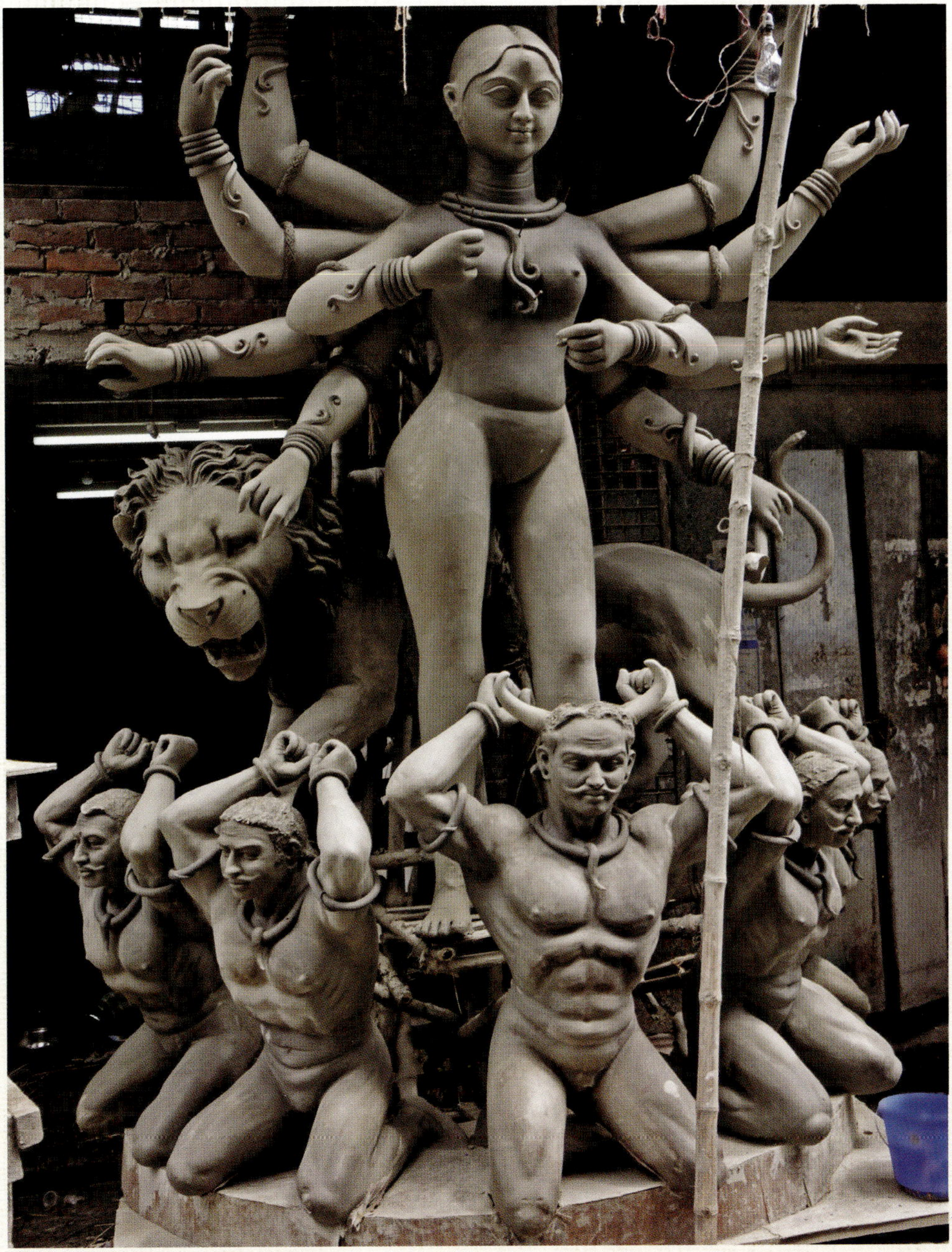

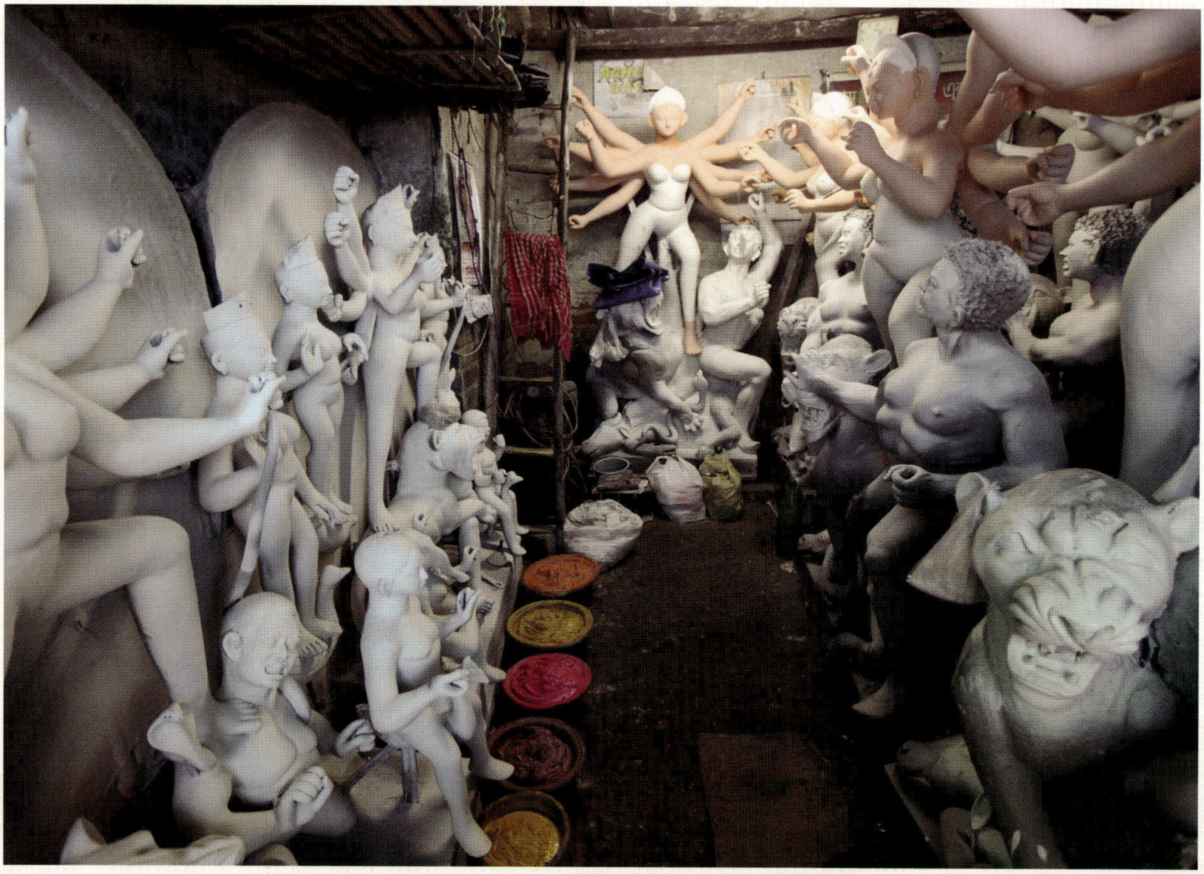

above and facing page: The various stages of painting in progress

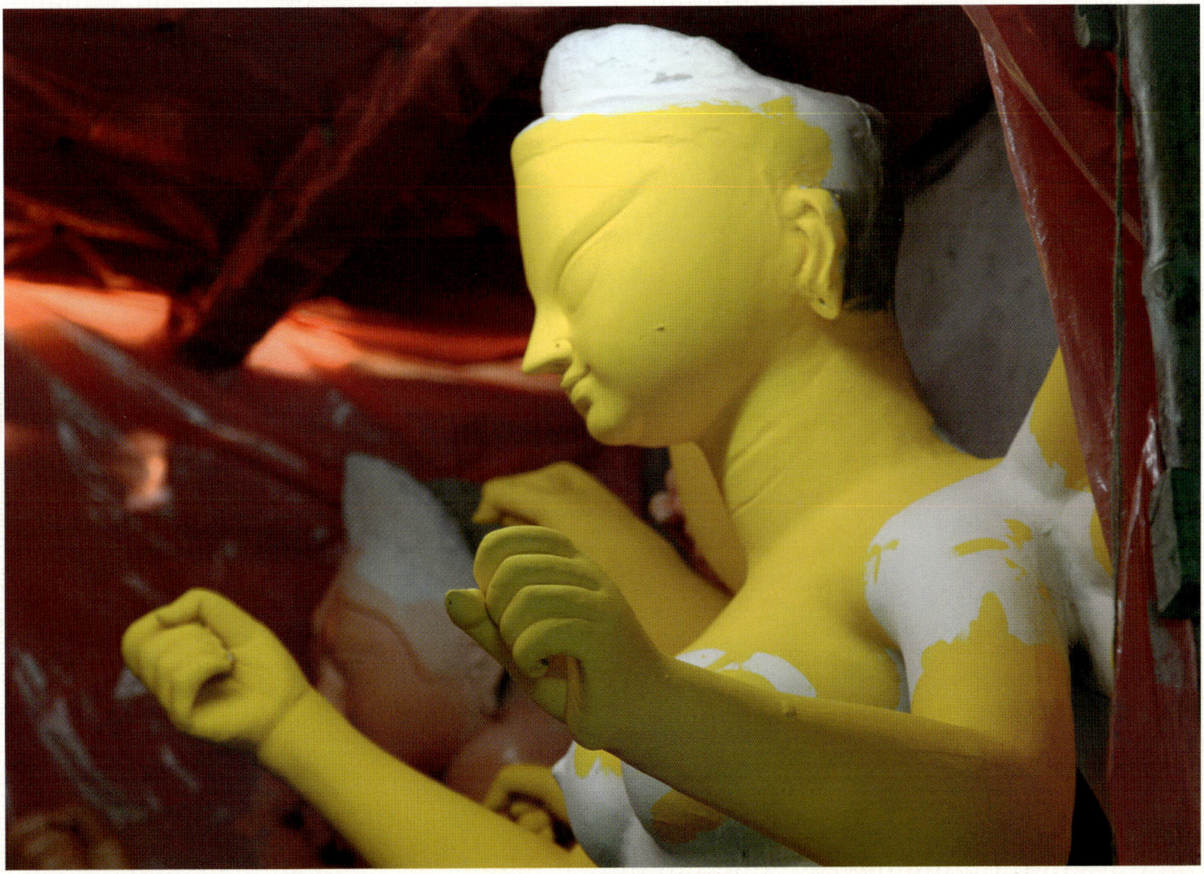

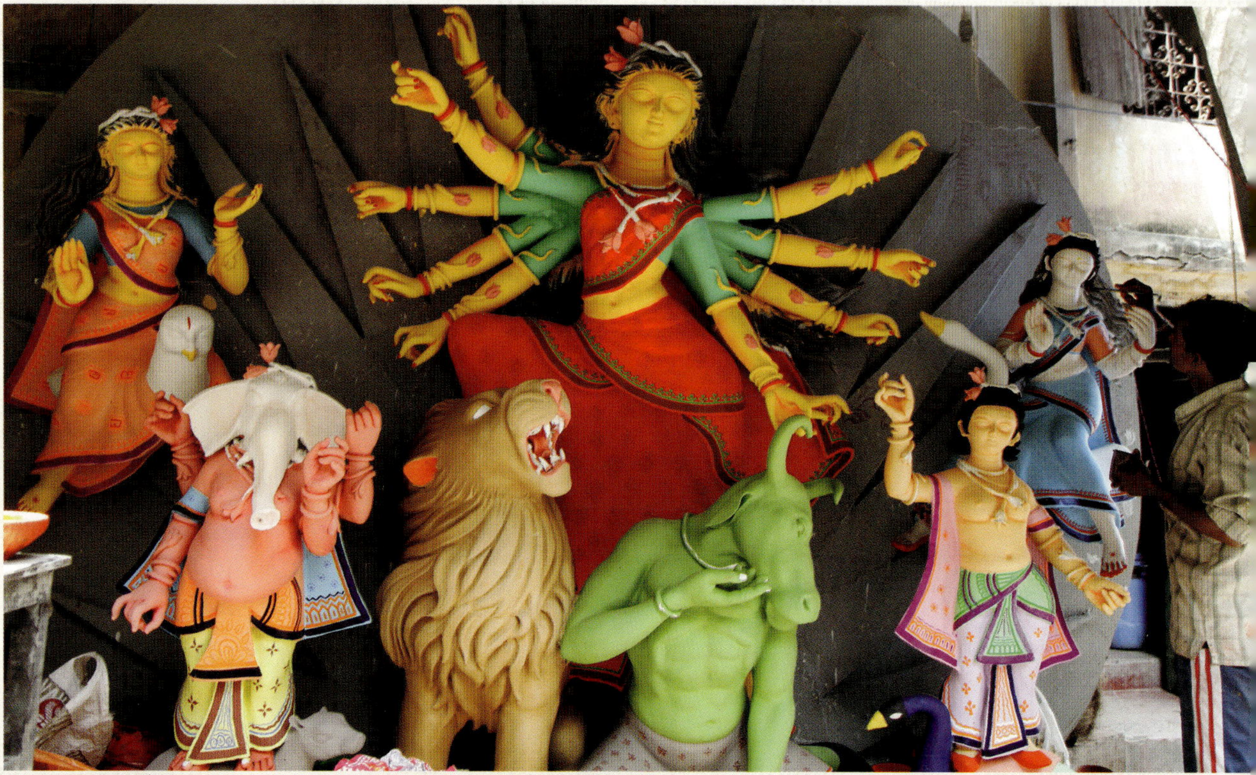

The eyes of the icons are about to be painted

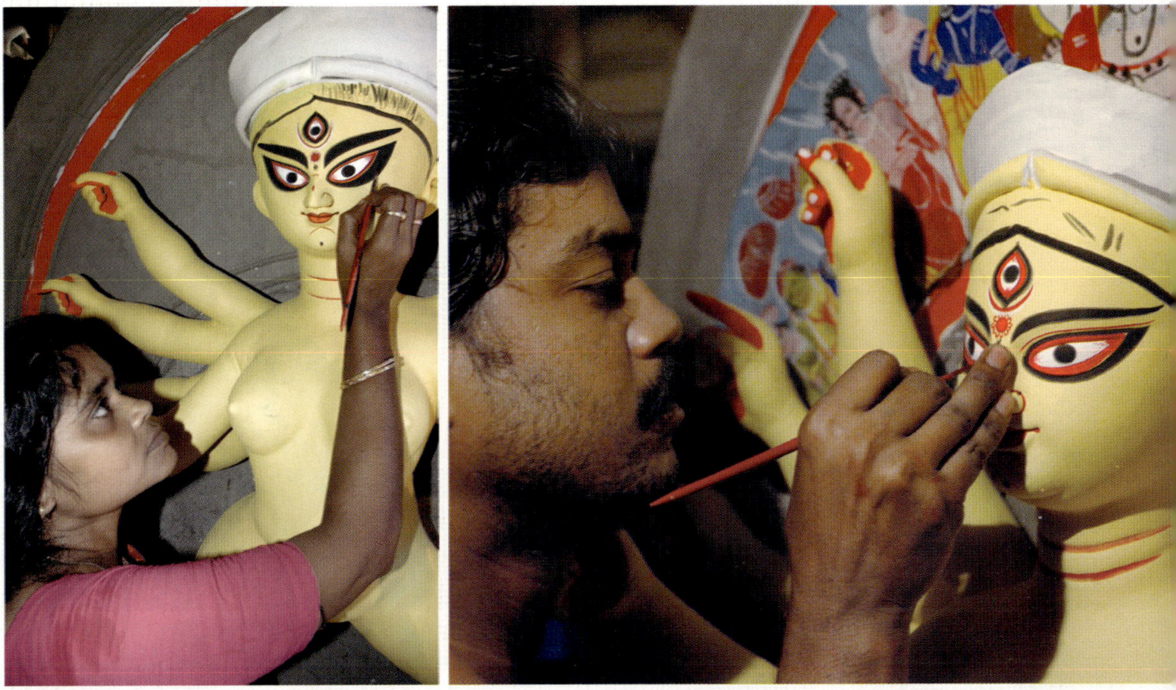

Netro-unmilon—the sacred act of painting the divine eyes

often with a modern spray gun for uniform distribution of paint, to represent the golden complexion of the goddess, to be followed by drawing of facial features, most importantly the eyes (through the ritual of *netro-unmilon*).

With the completion of modelling, the task of decorating the deities with costume and weapons begins. Traditionally, ornaments were made of shola pith, now coloured foils and synthetic materials rule. The costumes and jewellery are mostly bought ready-made from other craftsmen.

There are many special suppliers of divine apparel, jewellery and mythological weapons in and around the city and beyond. Most

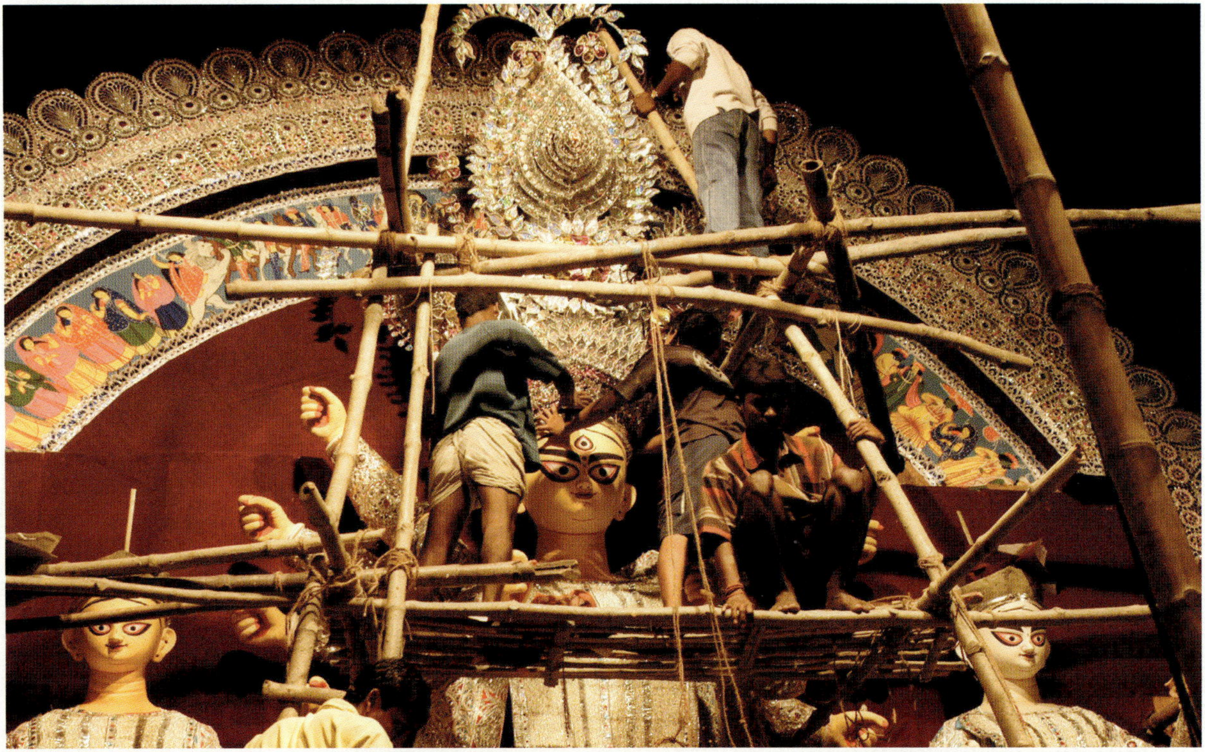

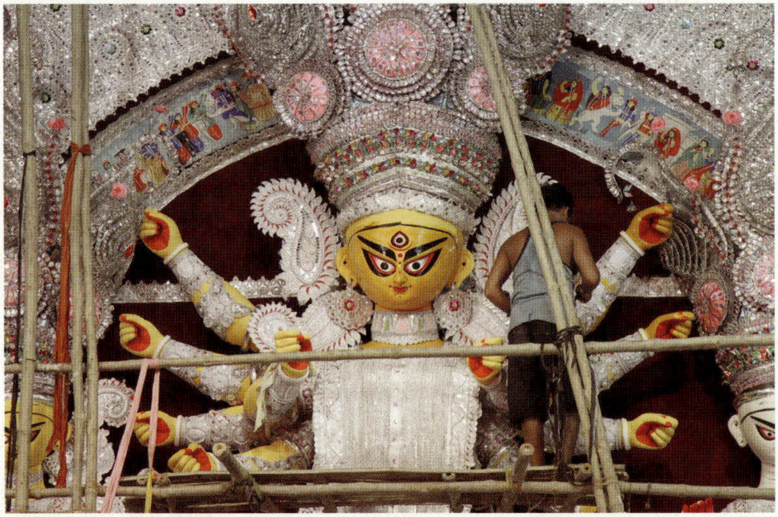

both: Huge icons require scaffolding for access during dressing and decoration

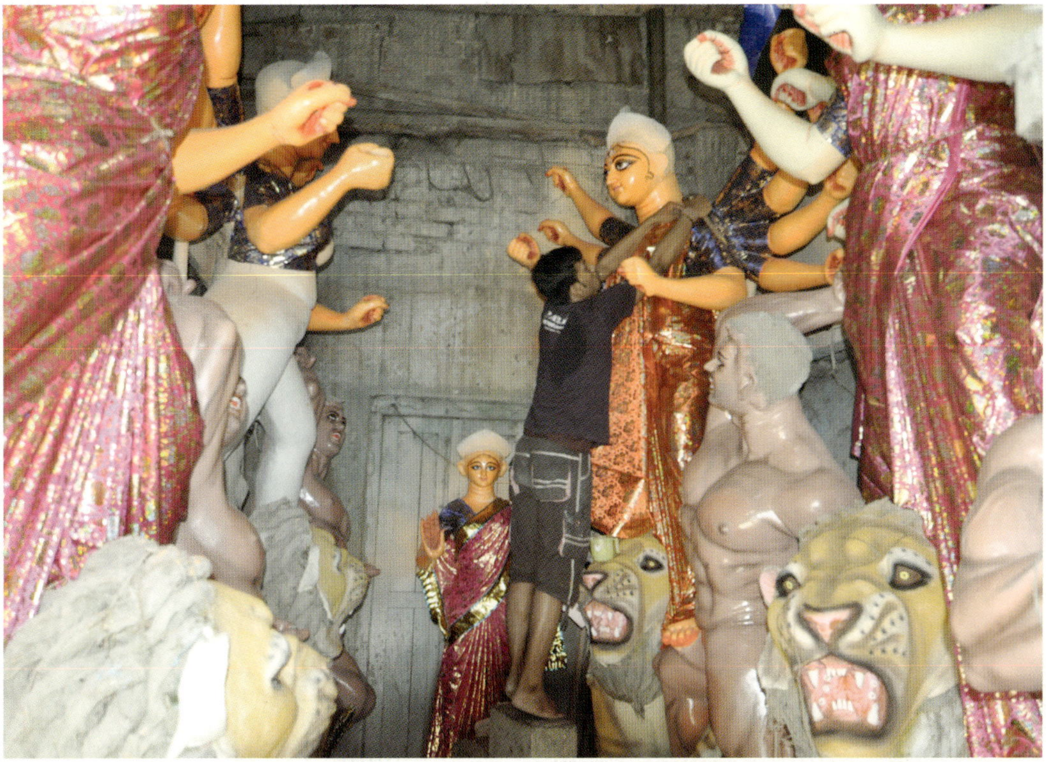

icon-makers have given up making these themselves, because retired jewellers, sequin and bead-workers, knick-knack makers and leather craftsmen have taken over this aspect as a lucrative seasonal work—and they are better at it.

Draping of the icons in progress

However, in some of the older traditional household Durga Pujas, real jewels are used to adorn the icons. These are later taken off before the immersion and preserved for the next year. With the surge of rampant commercialism in Kolkata, the last couple of years have witnessed the introduction of real gold and even diamond jewellery on some of the publicly displayed icons under strict security to advertise jewellers. This brings in the much-needed funding for the exorbitant cost of *barowari* (of the community) pujas.

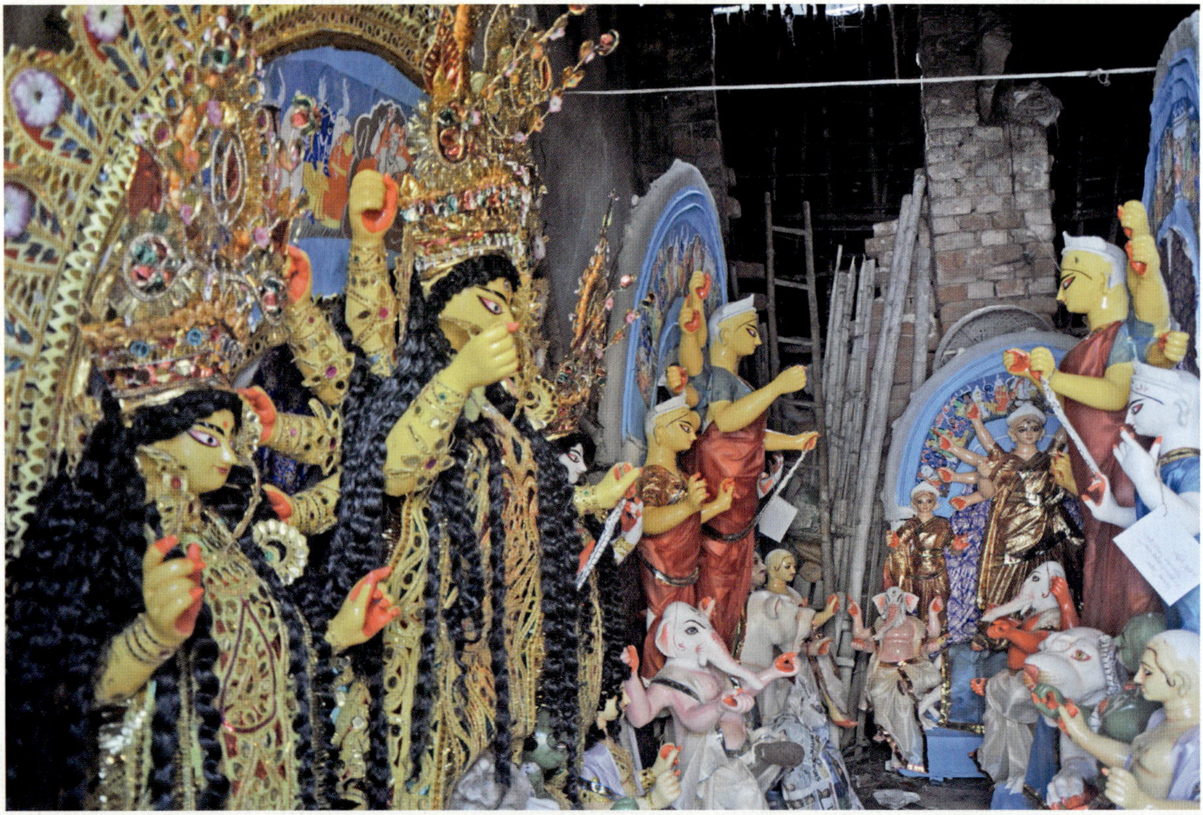

Finished icons waiting to be taken to the pandal while others await the finishing touches

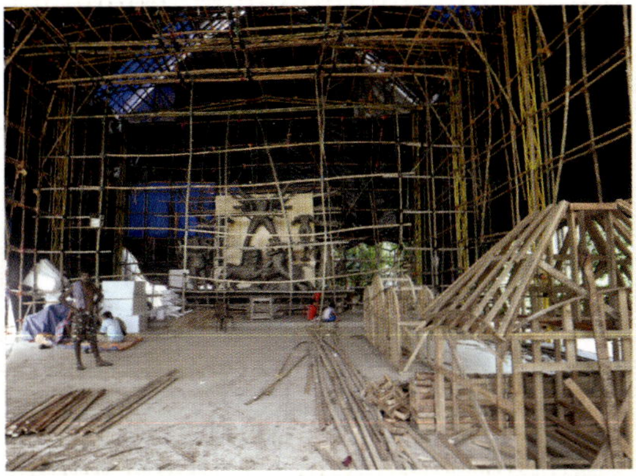 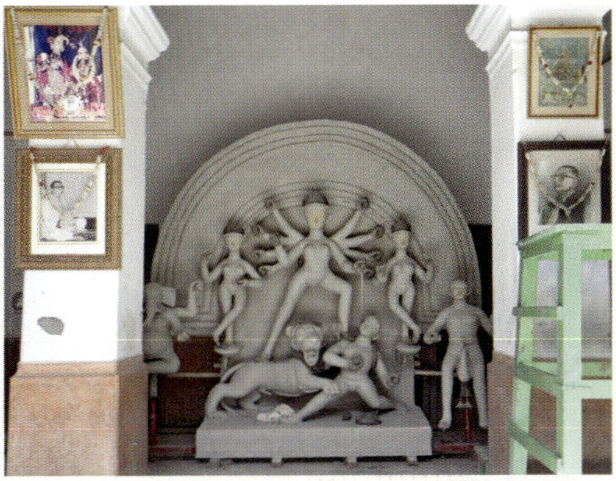

both above: In situ icon-construction in a large *barowari* pandal (left) and in one of the great ancestral houses (right)

Most of the artisans drape the icons themselves choosing the colour and the style of the garments with suggestions from clients. Some even employ special dressers with suitable skills.

Bengal has always relished dressing the gods with exquisite earrings, bangles and bracelets, amulets, chokers and necklaces, hair decorations like diadems and tiaras. So, the more extravagant these are, the more popular.

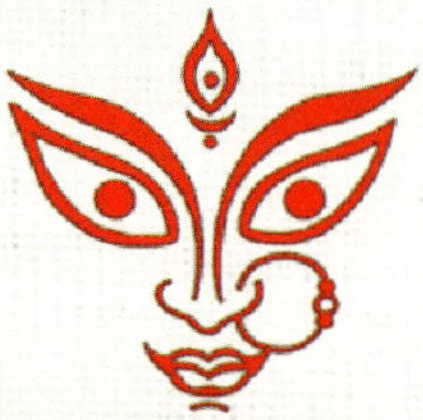

Over 250 years, the countenance of Durga has also undergone significant changes, reflecting contemporary taste.

Chalchitra, Shola Pith and the Changes

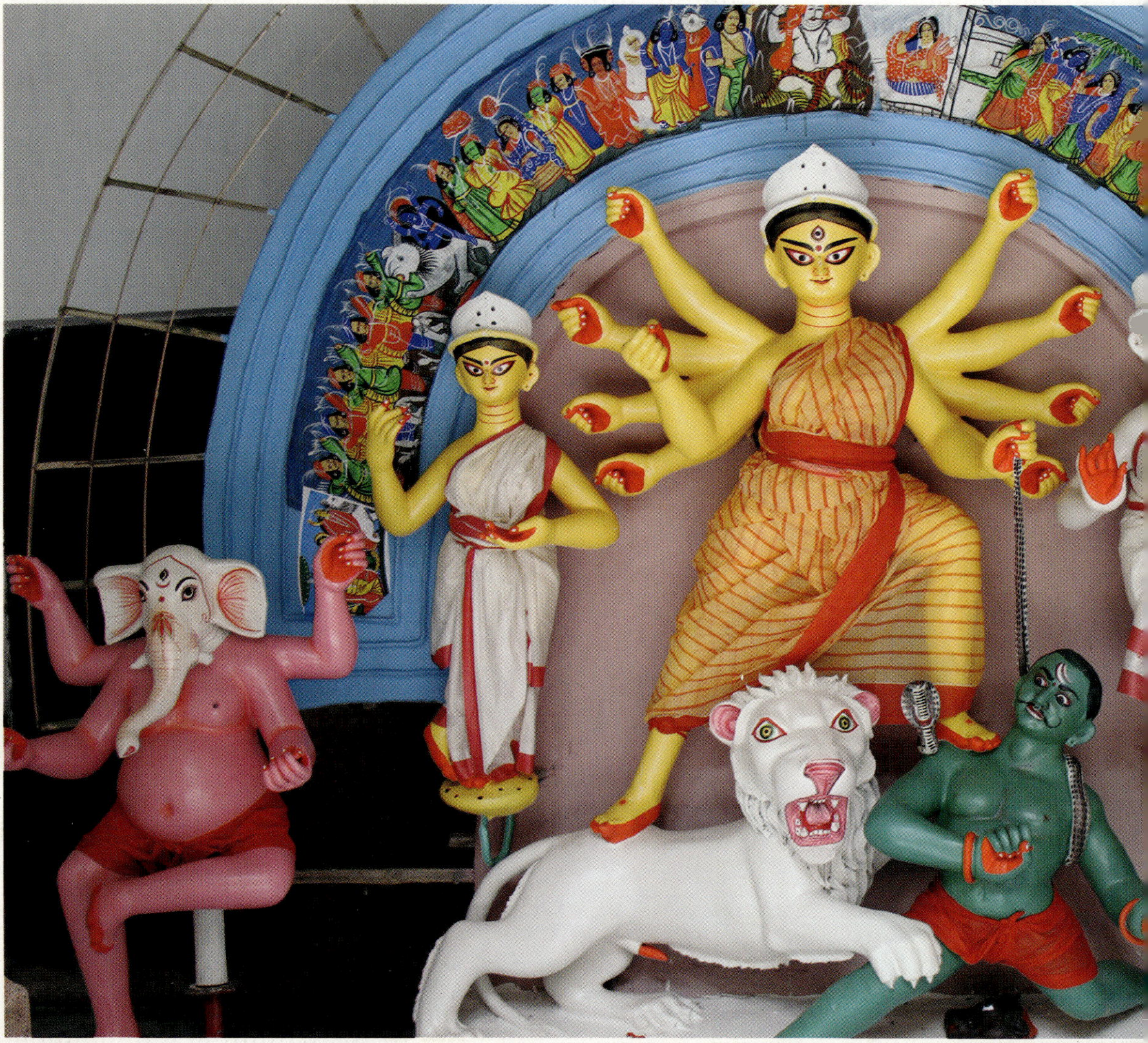

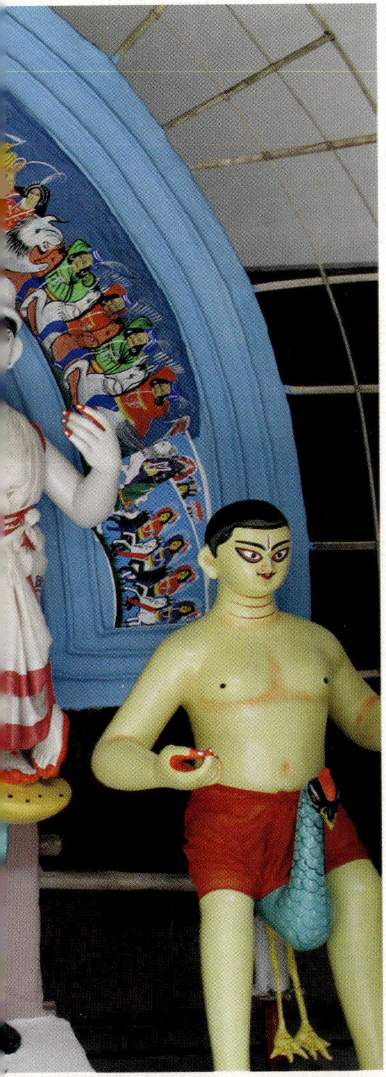

Chalchitra, an integral part of the entire tableaux

The word *chal* in Bengali means roof and *chitra* means picture; hence, the compound word *chalchitra* means 'picture on the roof'. The frescoes on the ceiling, for example.

Chalchitra generally refers to a semi-circular decorative wooden panel on a bamboo frame, set behind or above the icon, representing events and personalities from the divine universe. During the reign of the Pala dynasty in Bengal, between the late eighth and the twelfth centuries, when sculpture, architecture and painting flourished, *chalchitra* emerged as a formal style in sculpture like an arched frame of the statue. Much later it transfigured as an element of narrative folk art representing something like an aureole.

A variety of characters and events from the scriptures are portrayed across a hemispherical primed surface, over a coat of blue paint signifying the sky. For example, often there is Shiva with the moon and Brahma at the scene of the churning of the ocean. Its main function is to remind the spectator that Durga is a synthesis of other divinities and also to acknowledge the presence of other gods during veneration. The choice of the scenes painted varies, depending on family tradition. Some prefer pictures of divine domesticity with the goddess' abode on a hill, others marvel in celestial splendour of a miracle from the scriptures. To the devotees, *chalchitra* is a window into the divine reality in miniature. Pragmatically, it covers the unsightly bamboo frame, necessary to hold the heavy, solid icon, with an ornamental spin. Aesthetically, it is an architectural lunette.

For 180 years, from 1757 to 1937, the divine family of Durga with her two sons and two daughters was constructed within a single frame known as *ekchala*, meaning 'under one roof'. Most of the icons worshipped in traditional households, such as the one at the house of Nabakrishna Deb, are still single-framed. But in 1937, renowned icon-maker Gopeswar Pal (1892?-1944) broke away from this tradition of *chalchitra*. At Kumortuli's own *sarbojonin* (for all) puja, he installed the five icons of Durga, Lakshmi, Saraswati, Kartik and Ganesh separated from each other, realistically making Durga older than her children. Gopeswar had exposure to Western art and demonstrated the Indian clay modelling at the British Empire Exhibition at Wembley, London, in 1924. This manner of split-up figures continues today.

As the deities were split individually, the *chalchitra* became a problem, because the need to cover the bamboo work of each single deity still remained. In most cases, people improvised; they cut out religious images from illustrated books and calendars to stick on the frame to fill the small void, but they were uninspired and dull. Then Rakhal Pal, in the 1960s, reinvented *chalchitra* as an environmental setting for the gods. He painted aquatic Indian lotus and floating circular leaves on them. Lotus is regarded as a divine symbol of purity, so it was a highly appropriate design for a heavenly garden and patriotic too.

This also allowed others to play more freely with the possibilities of the *chalchitra*. Some began to use sections of ready-made

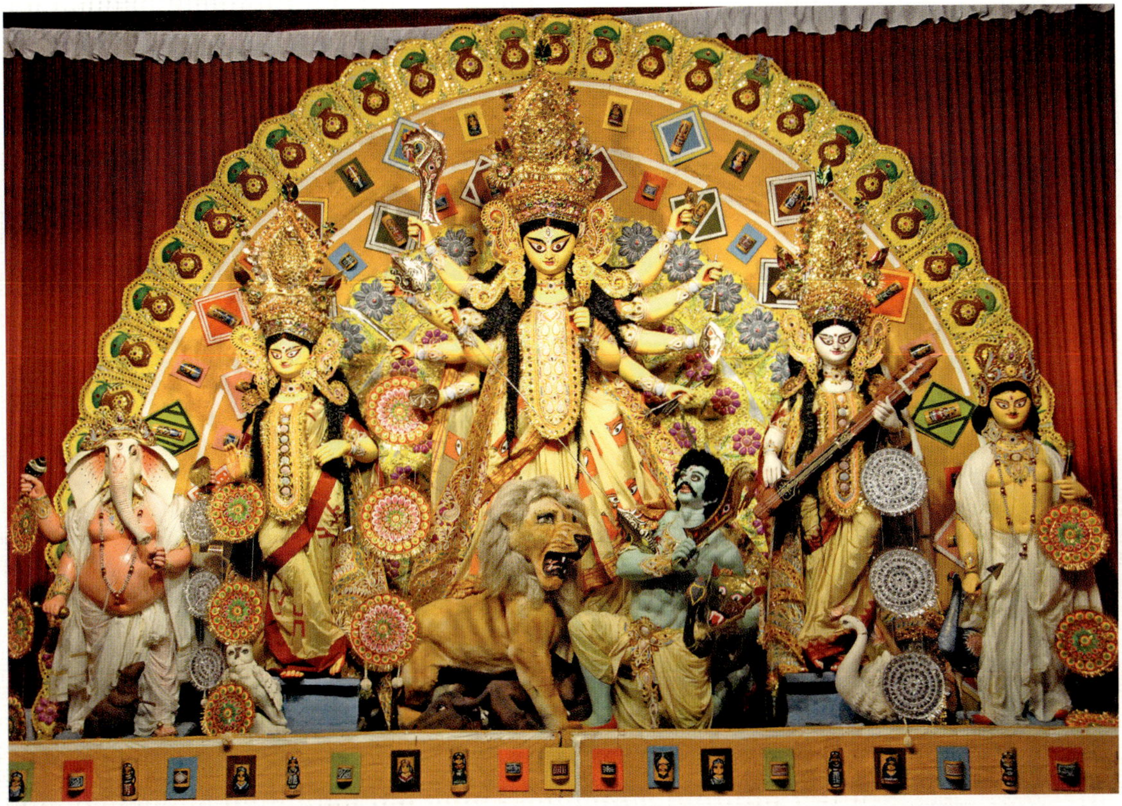

Ekchala murti

folk scroll paintings and shola pith or tinsel decoration; others extended the height of the icon's ceremonial crown to cover blank areas. Others have even put planetary scenes and landscapes on it. *Chalchitra* is certainly an integral part of the entire tableaux.

Shola pith is known in the West, from 1840s, as a material for pith helmet issued to the military personnel in the colonial service. But in India it has been traditionally used for decorative crafts.

The herbaceous shola plant grows in the marshy areas of Bengal, Assam, Odisha and South India. The diameter of the plant is about 4 cm across. When dried and after the brown outer skin is

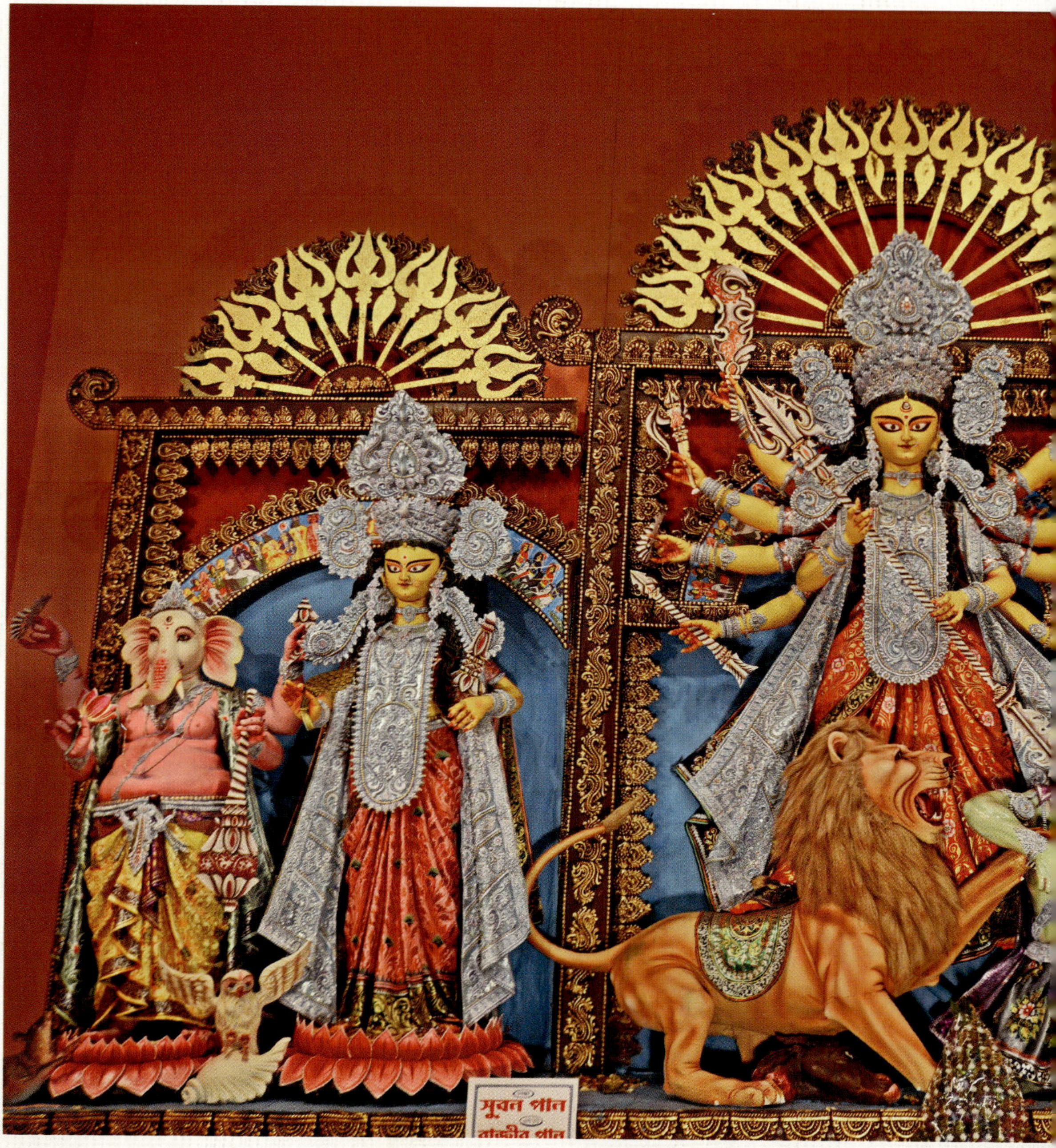

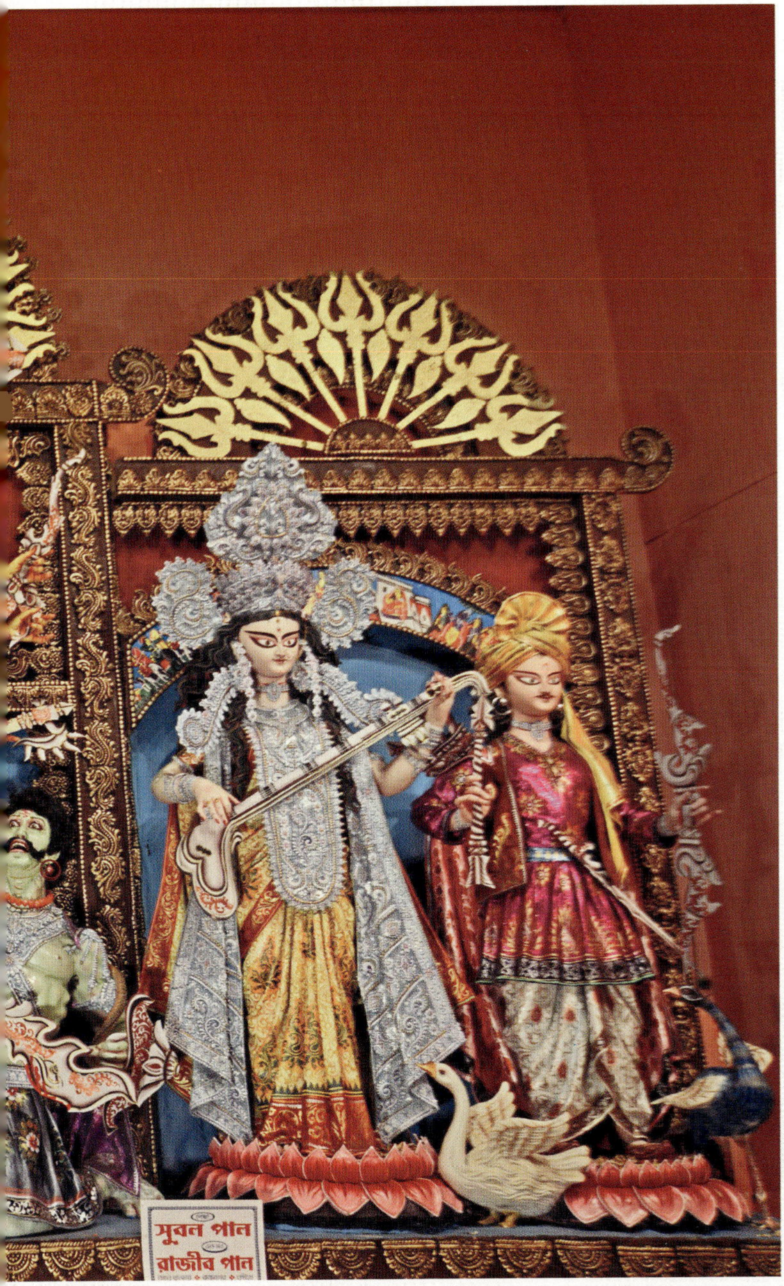

The more recent form of icons with separated *chalas*

removed, its milky white spongy pith can be cut and pressed into various shapes. The icon-makers of Kumortuli have been using it since the 1750s as an inexpensive locally grown material to decorate the gods they made. However, harvesting shola can be tricky and only the submerged section is used. The drying process needs close attention; otherwise, the white core will become grey and curled. Craftsmen use special thin and flat sharp knives to carve shola pith.

They can deftly slice a 4-6 cm long white stem into one 15-20 cm long strip, like peeling an apple from skin to core. With patience and meticulous skill they cut the strips to make flowers, birds, crowns, garlands and decorative hangings. Prior to the advent of polysterene, some craftsmen regularly built about a metre to two-metre high complete shola Durgas to ship abroad for expatriate communities.

All over Bengal, there are over 5000 artisans engaged in this enterprise. Most of them sell directly from their small workshops. You can pop into their tiny outlets in and around Kumortuli and watch them in action. They also make the essential Bengali wedding headgears (*sinthi* and *topor*) for the bride and groom and hanging garlands of decorative discs call *chandmala*—the garland of moon. At home, we had a realistic cockatoo mobile made of shola pith for years. These craftsmen learned and perfected their skills by making them from an early age. Before tinsel arrived from Europe and *daker saj* (ornaments sent by post) was conceived, all icons were decorated with shola pith finery.

Shola still continues to be used but now plastic beads and commercially produced golden and silver metallic materials woven into brocade fabric are also hugely popular.

Over 250 years, the countenance of Durga has also undergone significant changes, reflecting contemporary taste. However, the

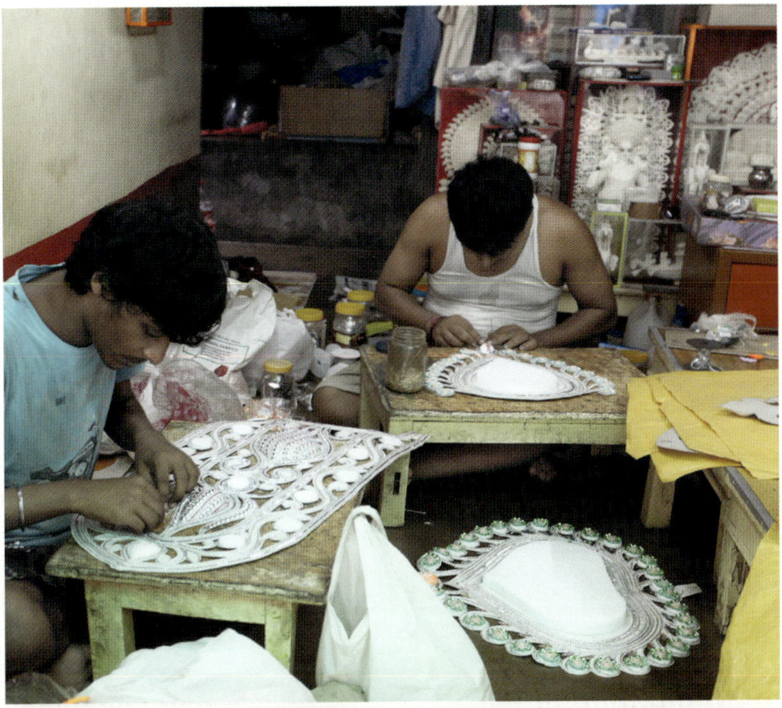

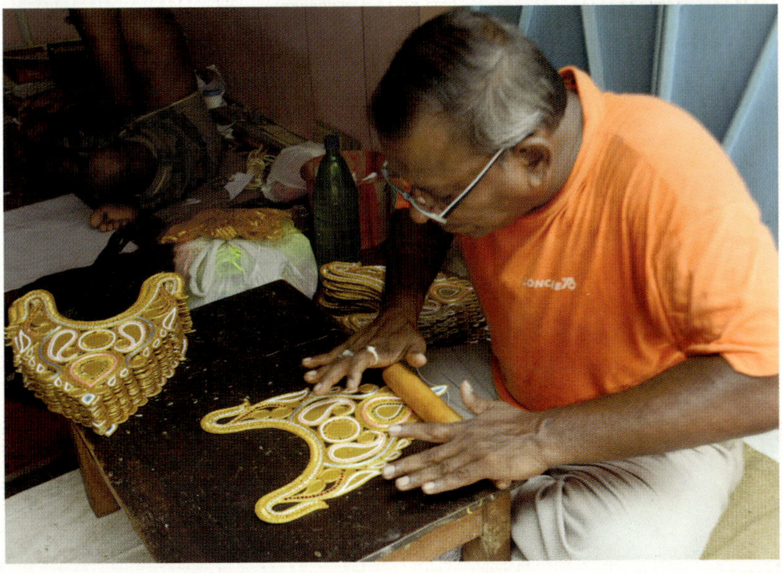

both: *Karigars* (artisans) making decorative ornaments for the icons

basic divine features with the third eye and a heart-shape face remain same. In the 1970s, especially after the Bangladesh war in 1974, the patriotic 'Mother India' Durga image evolved into a simple face, like a beautiful girl next-door, wearing a simple red-bordered sari with waist-length wavy black hair. But during the 1990s, she became richly decorated, perhaps reflecting trends towards free-market economy. After that, for a while, she often took the looks of popular Hindi movie stars. Now in 2013-14 she was seen sporting expensive real gold and diamond jewellery sponsored by big Indian jewellers.

From 2000 onwards, as India was becoming more confident of her place in the world, the artistic and cultural heritage of the country was also being reflected in the artwork. I remember seeing an icon dressed in *Kathakali* dance costume set in suitable South Indian scenery, and in another pandal the icon was constructed in the manner of Buddhist art.

Durga's mount, the lion, however lost his Indian appearance some time ago, gradually taking the appearance of the sculpted lion at the gate of the Raj Bhavan (Governor's house), which was originally installed by Lord Wellesley in 1802.

However, the facial expressions and postures of the demon, the lion and even

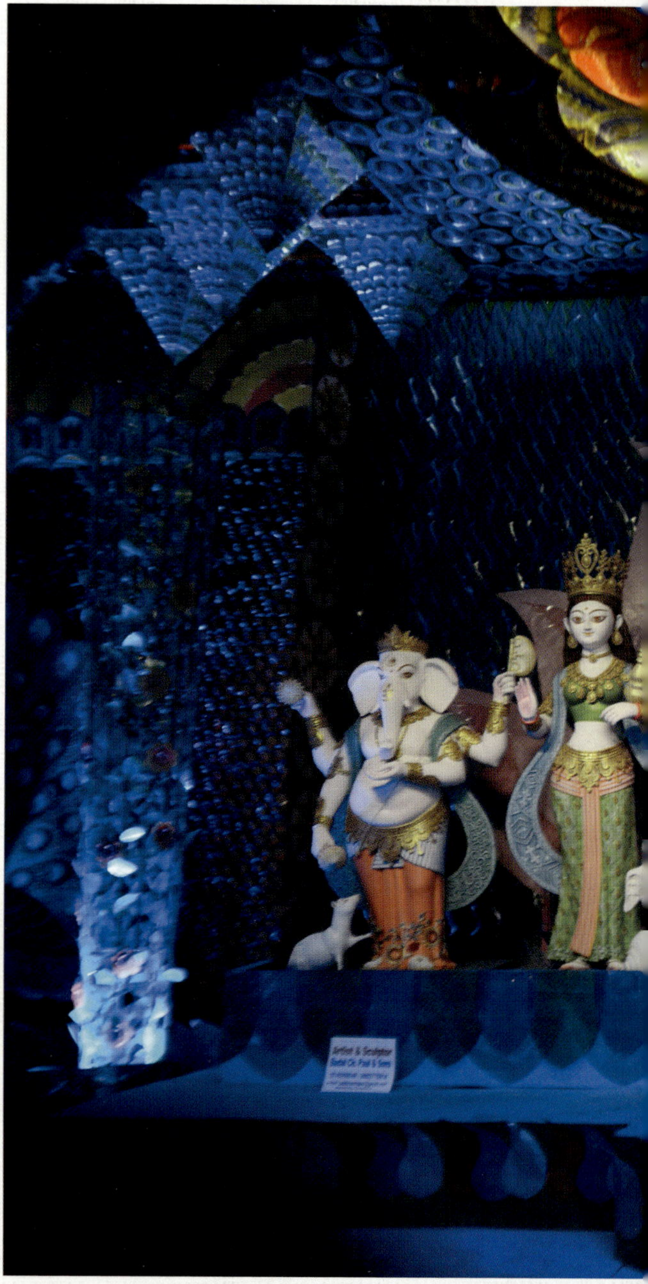

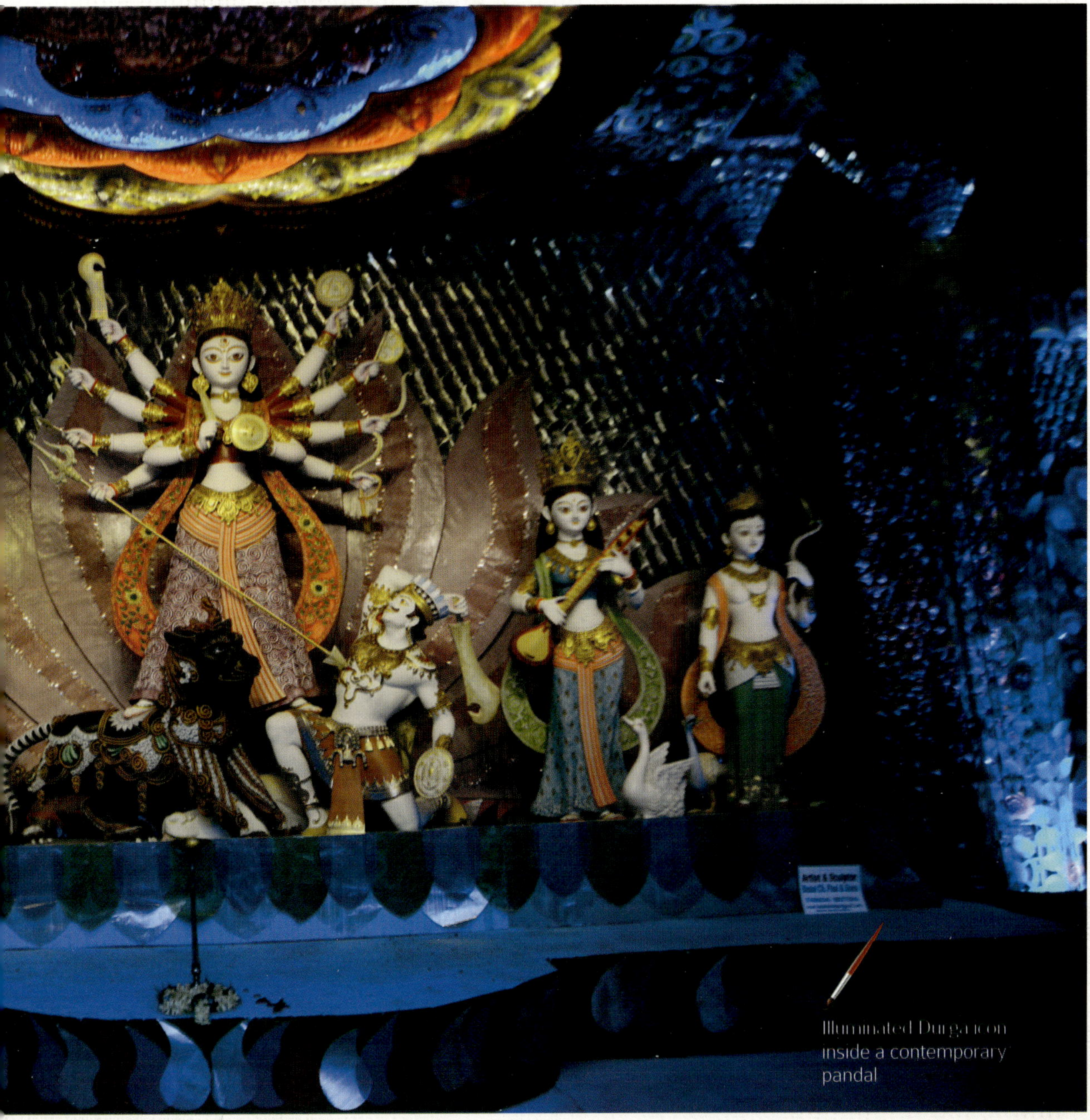

Illuminated Durga icon inside a contemporary pandal

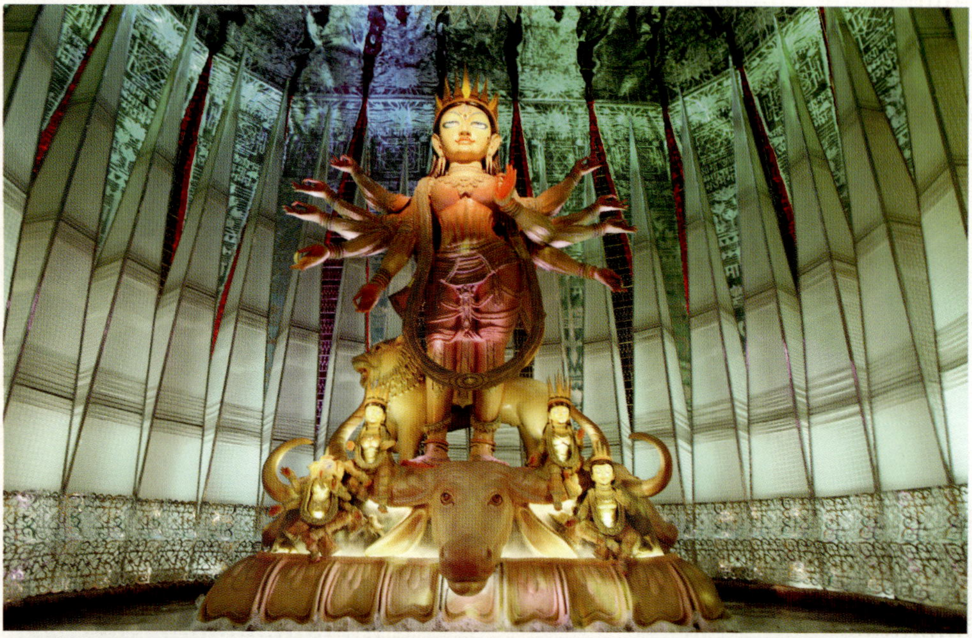

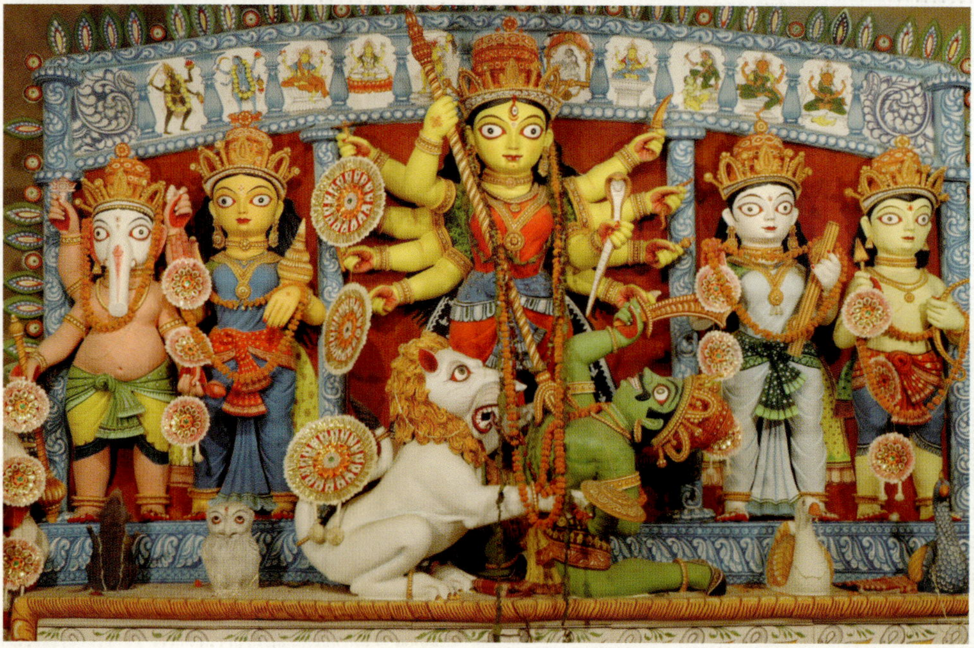

the goddess have become fiercer in recent years, perhaps reflecting the excess of violence of our age.

Since the situation of frequent electricity supply cuts has improved remarkably in Kolkata after the millennium, the illumination and imaginative lightings have begun to play an important part in Durga Puja displays everywhere. *Sarbojonin (for the masses)* pujas earmark a large budget to cover this. Many electricians now specialise in varieties of themed lighting and provide appropriate sound tracks for special effects. A couple of years ago, I saw one audio-visual display of a misty rainforest at a *sarbojonin* pandal. It was magical and dramatic with chirps of birds and the sound of gentle rain.

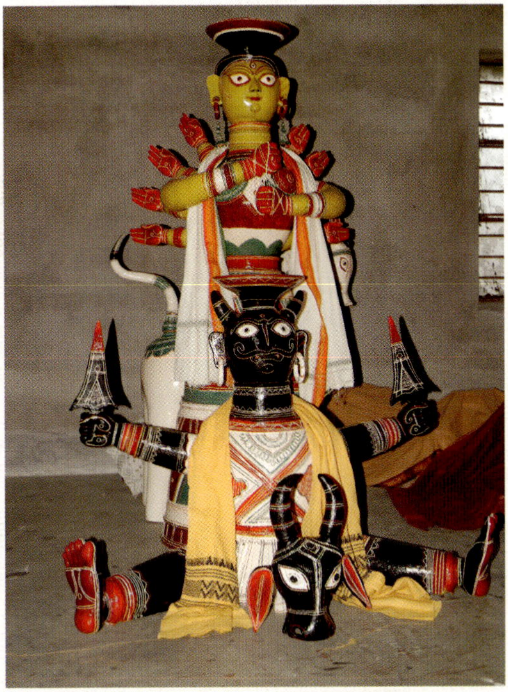

above and facing page: The icon of Durga has undergone many changes in form and conception over the years

The great Hindu epic, Ramayana, initiated the tradition of worshipping the goddess in September-October instead of spring.

The Origin and History of Durga Puja in Kolkata

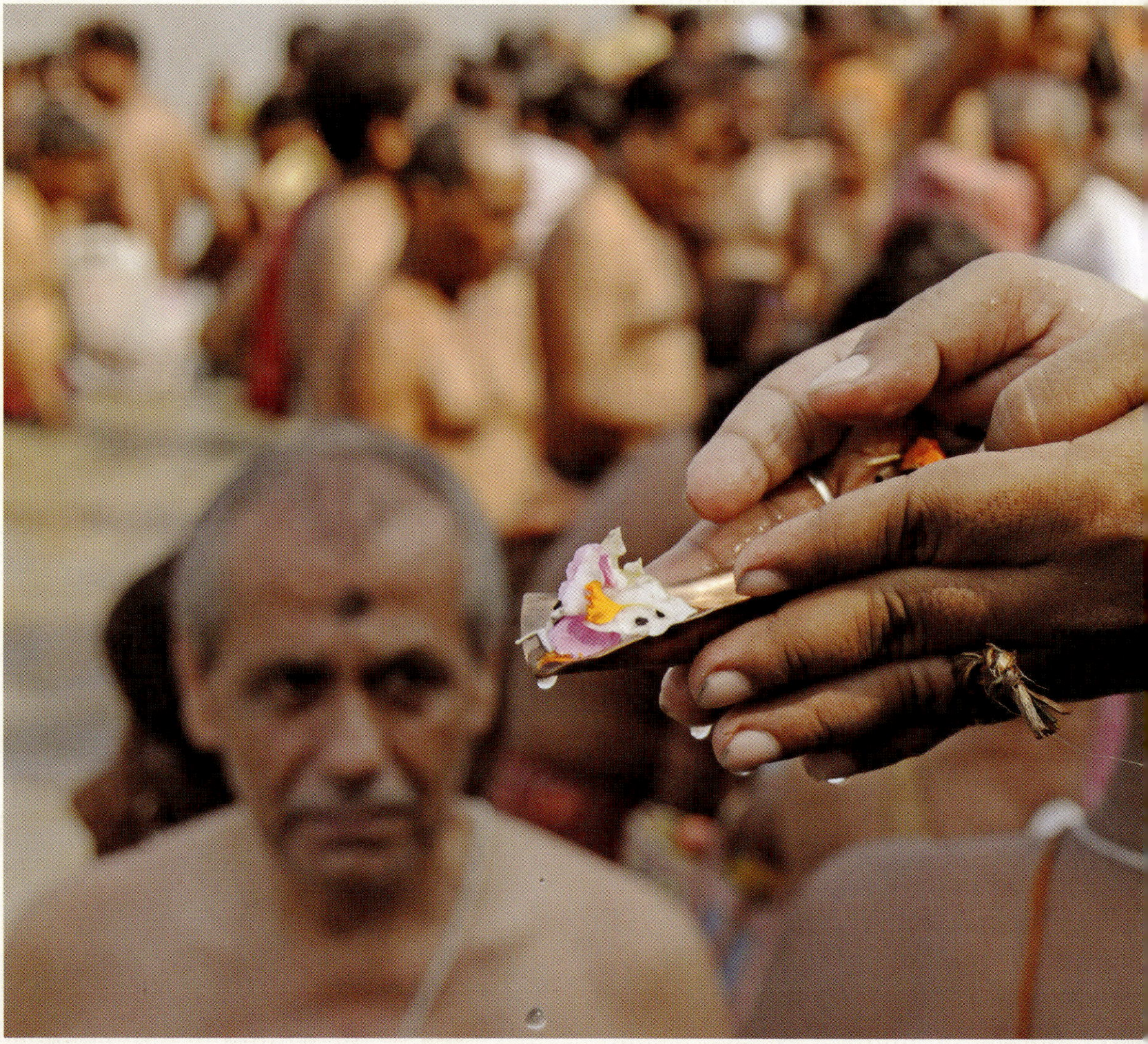

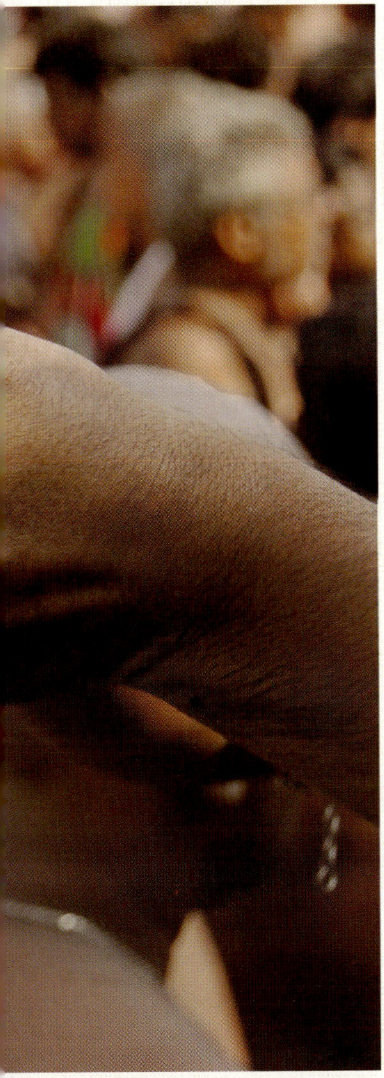

Tarpon in progress at Babughat, Kolkata on Mahalaya day

Durga Puja in Bengal celebrates the victory of good over evil.

The earliest image of the cult of Durga was found in northern India during first centuries of the Common Era. Her complete iconography as a buffalo-demon-slaying mighty goddess appears on a rock-cut panel at Mahabalipuram, also known as Mallapuram, in Tamil Nadu.

The great Hindu epic, *Ramayana*, initiated the tradition of worshipping the goddess in September-October instead of spring. According to *Krittivas Ramayana*, through pious devotion, Rama—the hero of *Ramayana*—invoked Durga untimely in autumn, prior to his battle with Ravana.

The dates of Durga Puja are not fixed but are calculated from the lunar calendar. The auspicious period stretches over ten days and rites begin on the first day called *Mahalaya*, when thousands of devotees arrive at the banks of river Ganga at dawn to pay respects to their ancestors through the ritual of *tarpon*.

Since the 1930s, on Mahalaya day, Kolkata radio has been broadcasting a dawn programme of readings from sacred texts

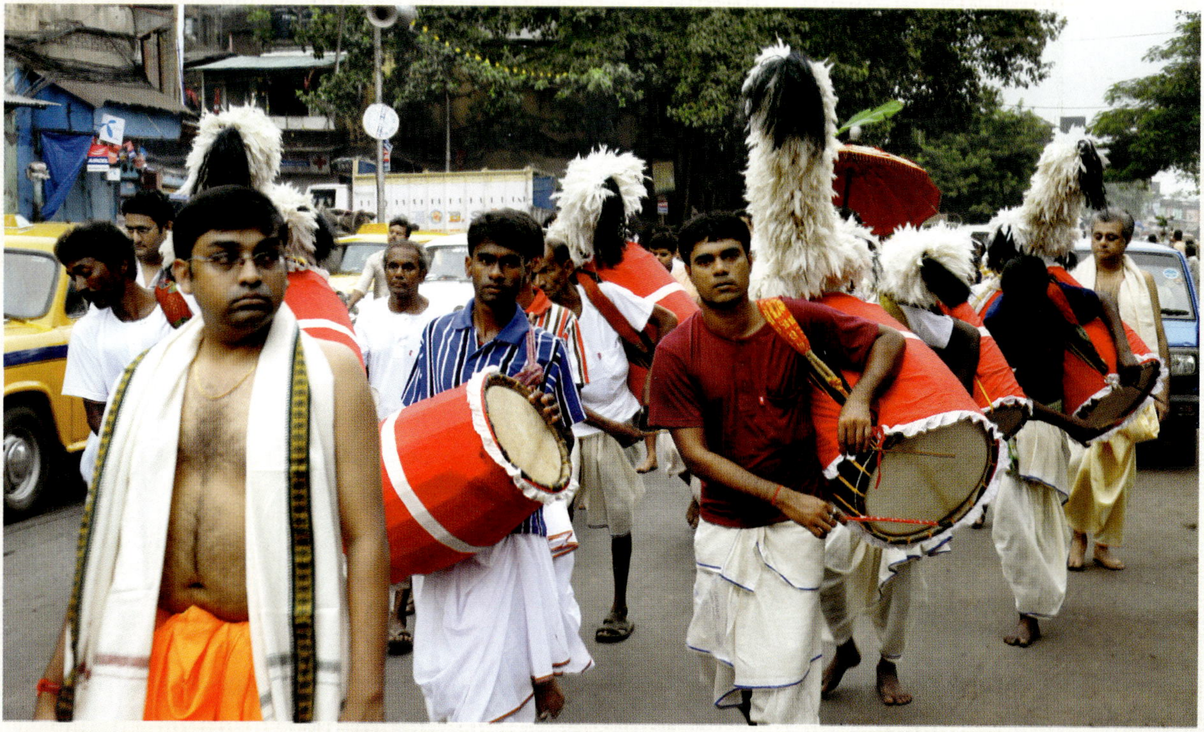

and songs in praise of Durga. Informally, this annual broadcast marks the day and sets the mood of the occasion. Now the TV channels also beam suitable visuals, and recordings of these are available for Bengalis living abroad. Augmenting the festive spirit, traditional drummers known as the *dhakis*, from neighbouring villages, amble around the streets beating their feather-decorated and quilt-covered drums, to protect them from sudden showers, along with folk singers singing traditional *agomonigan*—the songs of Uma's homecoming. Uma is an incarnation of Durga, to be clarified in a later chapter.

As mentioned earlier, in Hinduism, gods, like the humans, are often perceived as having many strands of personalities. Thus Durga, in her ceremonial appearance, is a fierce demon-slayer

The arrival of the *dhakis* enhances the festive mood

riding a roaring lion. But she is also Parvati, the wife of Shiva, and Uma, a married daughter, who annually visits her parental home in the plains of Bengal, from her distant mountain abode. She brings along her four gifted children—Lakshmi (goddess of wealth), Saraswati (goddess of knowledge), Kartik (god of valour) and Ganesh (god of success). The *agomonigan* welcomes the daughter home, and when, after the final five days of adoration she leaves, people tender her a fond farewell with the rituals of *bishorjon* and *bijoya*. Devotees often get emotional that day and shed tears of parting as they see the icon submerged in the Ganga.

The forefathers of Raja Krishna Chandra Ray, mentioned earlier, seem to have conducted the first recorded Durga Puja in Bengal as a private act of worship. In 1610, before the founding of the city of Calcutta, the family of Sabarna Chaudhuris of Barisha-Behala—the original landowners of the place—held the oldest Durga Puja of the city. It is still held in traditional manner in their old elegant *thakurdalan*.

During the second half of the eighteenth century, several affluent Bengali families began hosting Durga Puja in their grand houses with much pomp and spectacle, vying against each other. Some of them even ignored religious scruples, as they welcomed Muslim musicians and nautch girls to dance, and offered their European guests wine with beef and ham for dinner.

One such Durga Puja was held in October 1757 at the house of Raja Nabakrishna Deb at 36, Nabakrishna Street in the north of the city. The story goes that after his recent victory at the battle of Polashi (Plassey), Clive wanted to make a grand gesture of thanksgiving, but the only church in Calcutta, St. Anne's, had been demolished during the siege of the city. Clive consulted his Indian tutor and advisor, Nabakrishna Deb, who proposed that he make an offering at the feet of Durga at his house. From the financial reward received for his service to the East India Company, he hurriedly but purposefully constructed an impressive *thakurdalan* and a dance hall, for the pleasure of Clive and his associates, hosting the legendary 'Company Puja'.

254 years after the event, during the Durga Puja in 2011, the family made a public denial of the story through a poster, stating that it is but a 'baseless gossip' of 'idle and ignorant minds of biased individuals'. However, ample historical records survive in British archives to testify the close financial and political collaboration between Clive and Nabakrishna Deb during and after the battle of Plassey. As H. E. A. Cotton noted in his book *Calcutta Old and New*:

> It is one of the inevitable results of a foreign occupation that the history of modern India as written by Englishmen – and no one else has cared to write it – takes little account of the Indian helper whose aid has been essential, and whose advice and knowledge has been invaluable, to the men who built up the fabric of English rule. Nowhere, perhaps is this reticence of history more marked than in the case of Maharaja Nubkissen, the friend and counsellor of Clive and Hastings who beginning life as the Persian tutor of the latter, rose to be the Company's interpreter and crowned career as their political *banyan* ... Yet he was no ordinary man, and the influence and power wielded by him during the thirty years which precede his death in 1797 was extraordinarily large. (Cotton p.353)

Indeed, Nabakrishna Deb was a dynamic personality who introduced music, poetry and other artistic forms of entertainment as cultural elements of the festivity. He was a patron of intellectual activities and held meetings of contemporary learned men at his house. Musicians like Harekrishna Dirghangi, Netai Kabial and others were regularly invited to perform in his music room. He donated money to diverse institutions irrespective of their religious allegiances. As a broad-minded philanthropist, he funded a madrasa in Calcutta and bequeathed land for St. John's church.

As time went by, Durga Puja evolved into more of a public event than an exclusive affair of a few affluent families. The trigger was around 1760s, soon after the Company Puja, when a group of 12 Brahmins were banned from participating in a particular Durga Puja at a family home. They instantly decided to hold their own puja and fund it collectively. This was the beginning of a communally subscribed Durga Puja. The word *barowari* in colloquial Bengali literally means 'of twelve chums'. Now *barowari* stands for all kinds of joint ventures. *Sarbojonin* is the posh synonym of *barowari* . Annually, over 2000 Durga Pujas in Kolkata alone are financed by public donations.

Worth noting here, as the growing idea of nationalism took some hold in Bengal around the mid-1880s, the image of Goddess Durga was reinvented as a symbol of Mother India inspired by a literary work.

The Bengali novel *Anandamath* by Bankim Chandra Chattopadhyay, serialised in a leading Bengali literary monthly in 1881-82, depicted Durga as the patron deity of liberated India. The novel became such a patriotic touchstone that the British soon banned the book. It remained banned till the end of British rule in August 1947.

The first publicly subscribed *barowari* Durga Puja was organised in Kolkata by Bhowanipore Sanatan Dharmotsahini Sabha in 1910, at Balaram Basu Ghat Road, Bhowanipore. Inspired by *Anandamath*, the organisers wanted to make the people identify motherland Bengal with the persona of Goddess Durga. This, they felt would give a religious fervour to the growing nationalistic feelings. The group also provided a public platform, for displaying the art of stick wielding, fencing and wrestling. They were determined to foster a martial spirit, as the youth prepared to fight the British rulers. One such puja, organised by a local fitness club, still goes on in Simla Street, north Kolkata. There, in 1939, the legendary nationalist Subhas Chandra Bose, unveiled a 20-foot-high image of Durga.

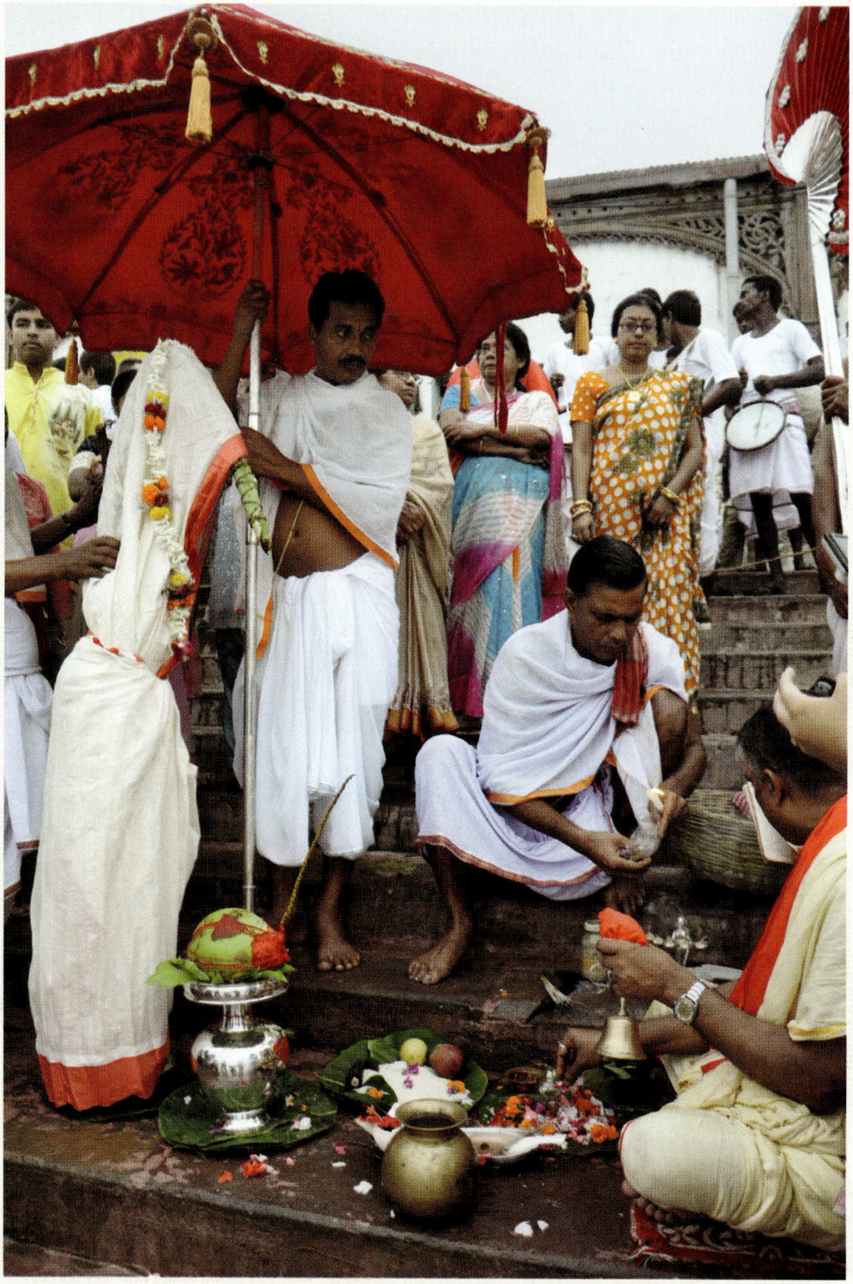

The late writer Sunil Gangopadhyay recorded in 1944, after Subhas Chandra Bose had secretly fled from India in disguise, that the Gangopadhyay family secretly arranged to get an icon made of the holy family of Durga where one of the icons would have the face of Subhas and a likeness of a British military officer as the demon mauled by her lion. This was meant to be a tribute to Bose's patriotic heroism. Somehow the police soon came to know of this. They seized the entire image just a couple of days before the ceremony. In desperation, the family took recourse in the tradition of *ghot* worship instead.

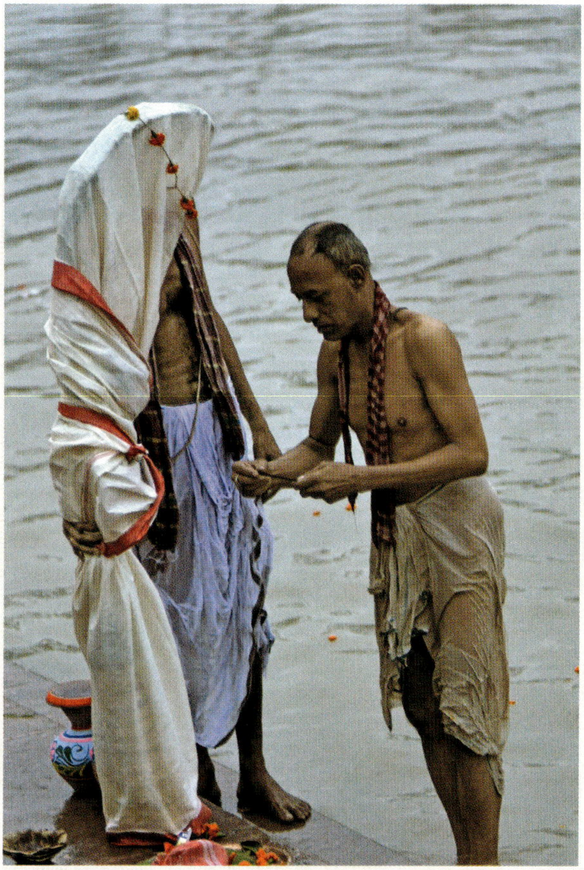

The five-day ceremony of Durga Puja follows an orderly structure, starting with *bodhan*, the invocation of the goddess with incantation, and the bathing of *kolabou*, the ritual washing and dressing of a banana plant signifying purification. The following three days are marked with the acts of *pushpanjali*, when the devotees offer the goddess flowers with chanting, and *arati*, her veneration with prayers and lighted lamp. The final day holds the ceremony of *sindurkhela*, when married women playfully daub vermillion powder in the parting of each other's hair celebrating Uma (Parvati)'s happy marriage to Shiva. The afternoon and evening of this day are reserved for *bishorjon*, immersion of the icon in the river in order to send the goddess back to her husband in Mount Kailash.

above and facing page: Ritual bathing and draping of banana plant (*kolabou*)

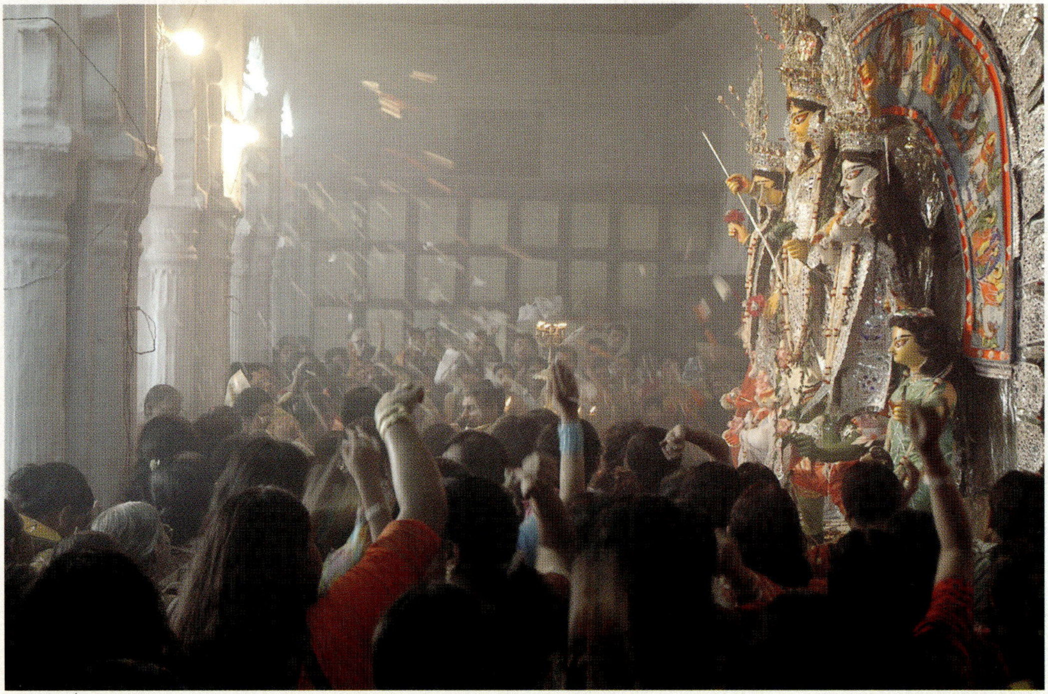

Pushpanjali—veneration with flower

facing page: The joyous ceremony of *sindurkhela*

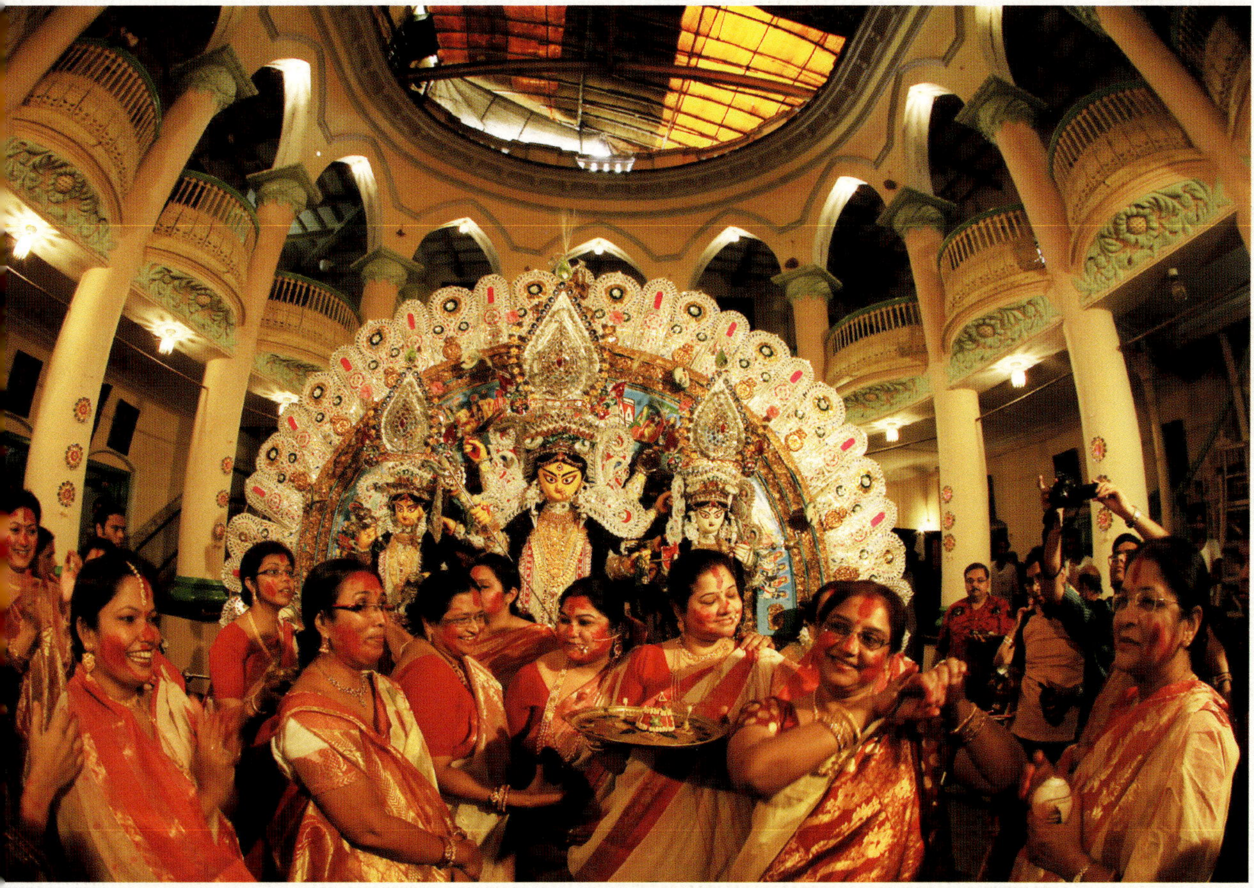

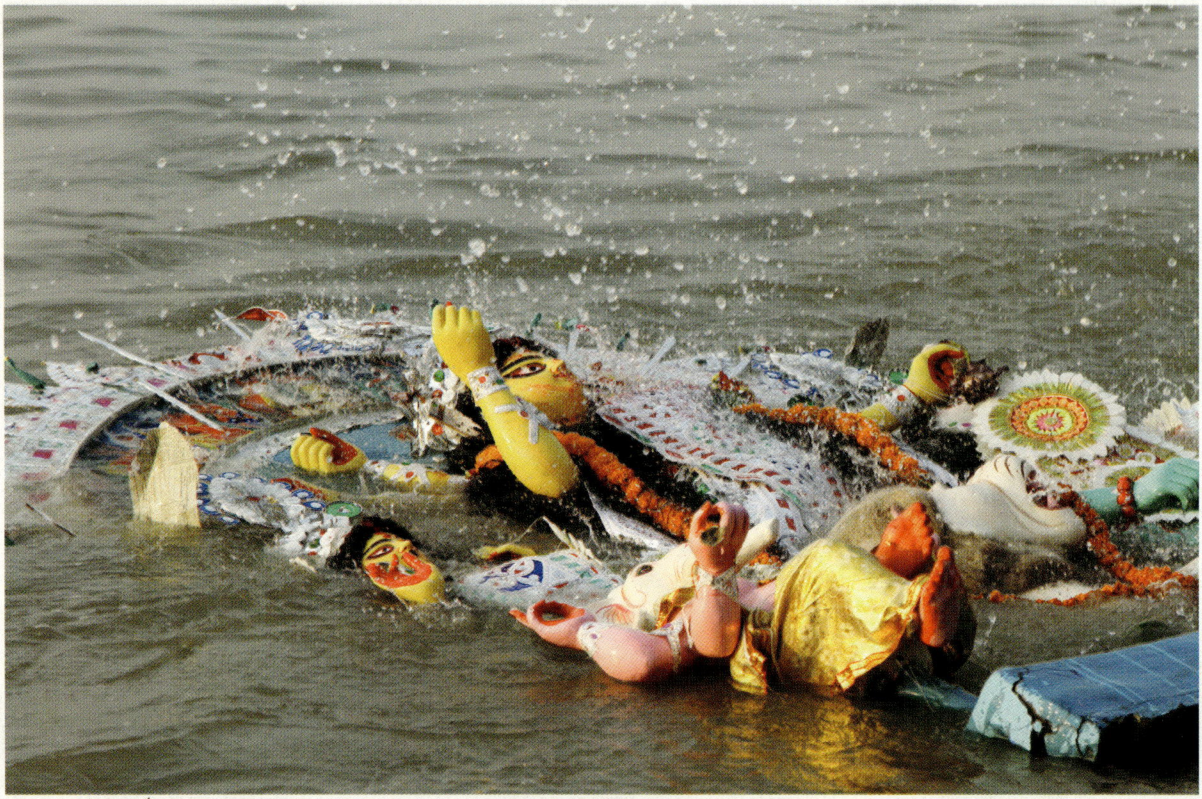

above and facing page: *Bishorjon*—immersing the icon in the river

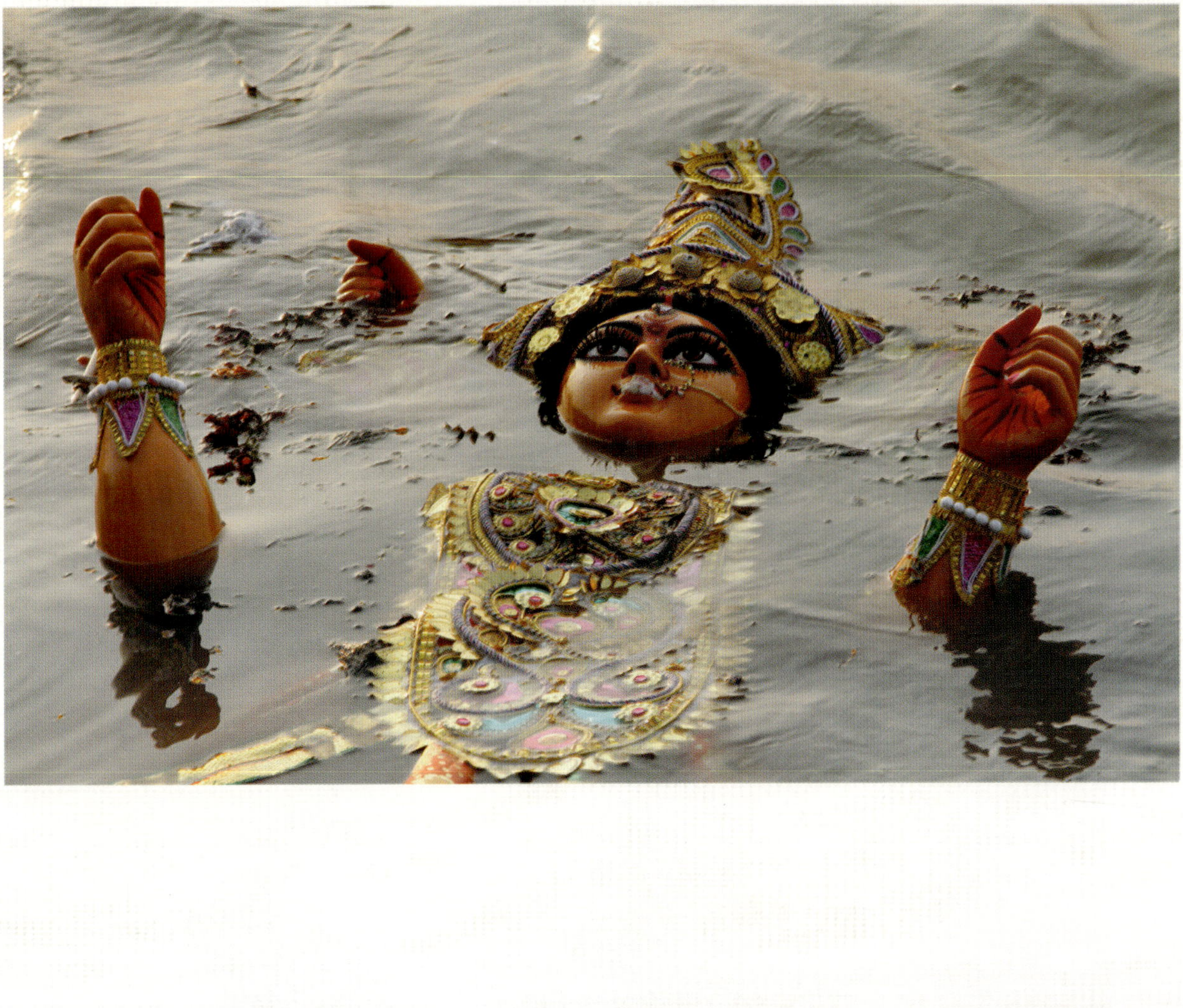

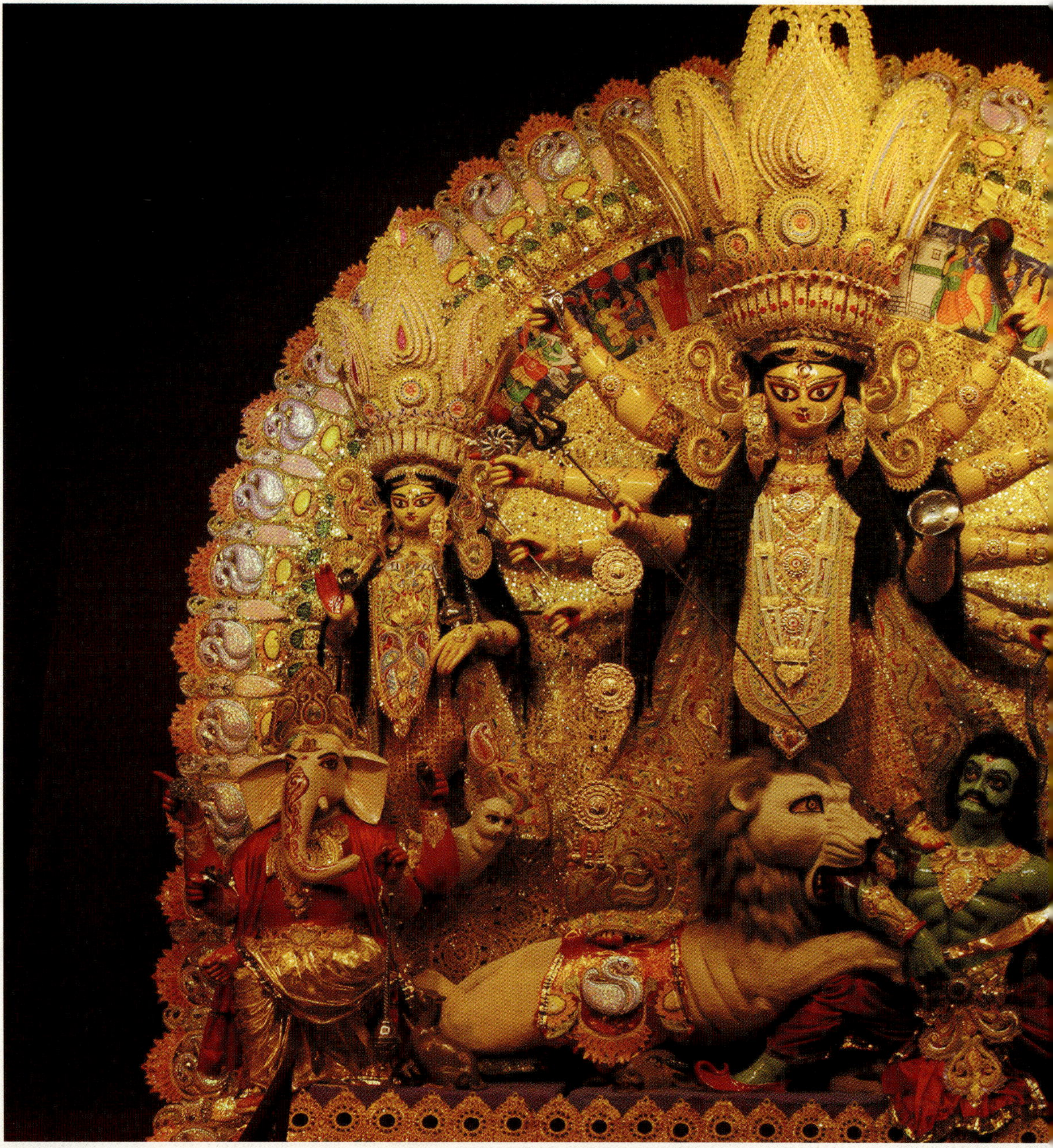

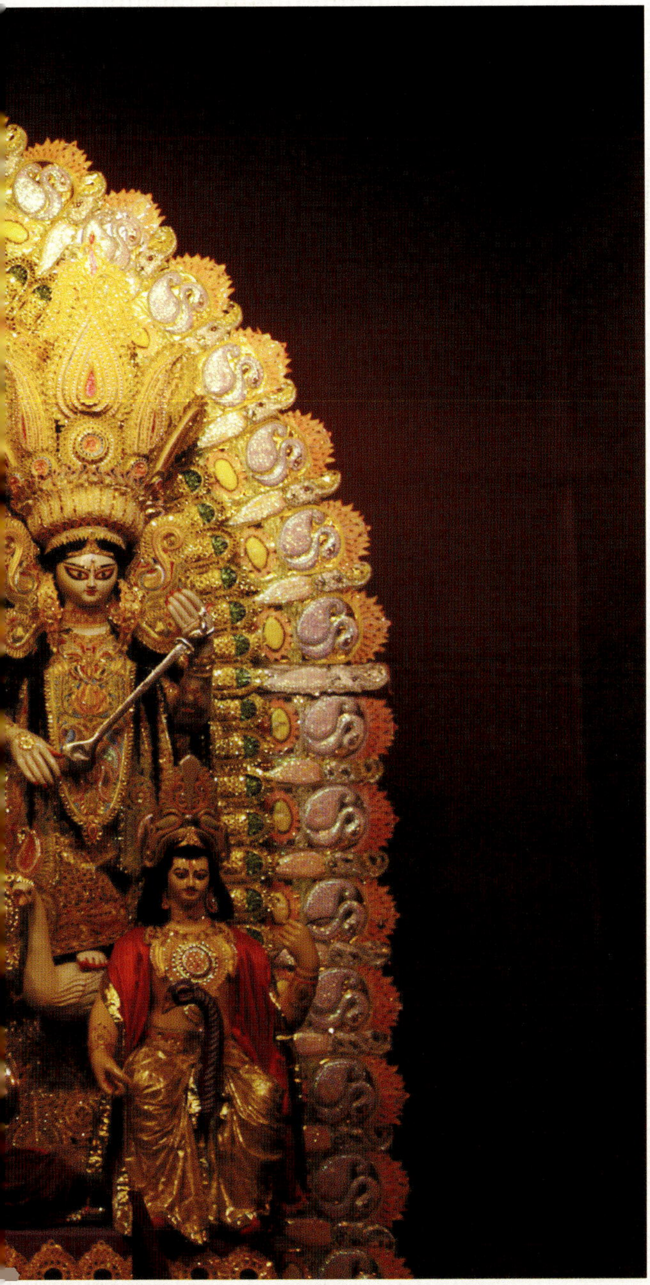

Since Independence in 1947, Durga Puja has slowly changed into more of a carnival than a religious festival. The temporary shrines known as pandals, to house the icons, pop up all over the city. The novelty and innovativeness of their design and decor induce a magical spell in the city.

On the day of *bishorjon*, devotees often imagine the divine eyes of the goddess to appear tearful, given her imminent departure

Durga Puja in September-October
is Kolkata's most important festival
culminating in a five-day veneration
of the divine family, when the
city hosts a great carnival with
illumination, music and jollity.

Durga Puja

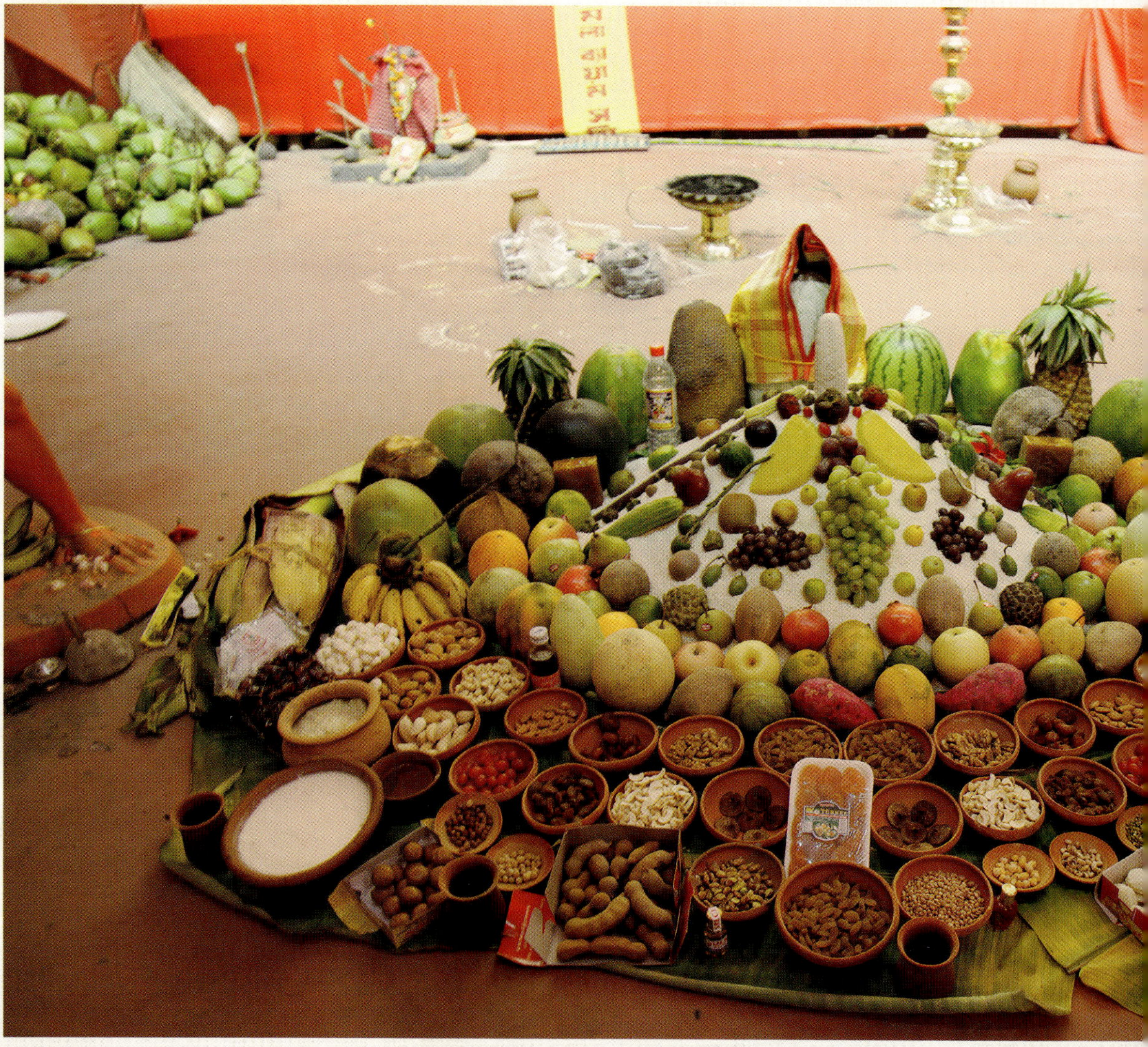

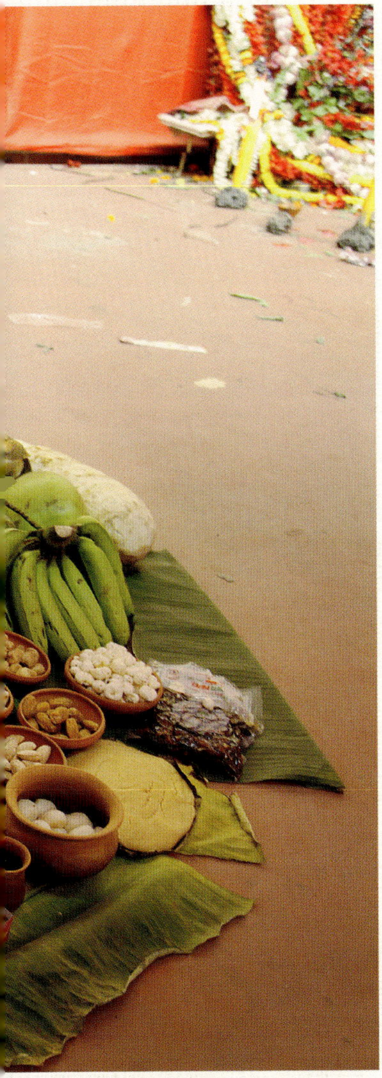

left: An elaborate spread of offering for the divine

below: A *purohit* performing puja at a *barowari* puja pandal

'Durgo' means fortress in Sanskrit and the word Durga, as its derivative, metaphorically stands to mean 'the invincible'. Durgo was also the name of a demon defeated by the goddess.

Durga Puja in September-October is Kolkata's most important festival culminating in a five-day veneration of the divine family, when the city hosts a great carnival with illumination, music

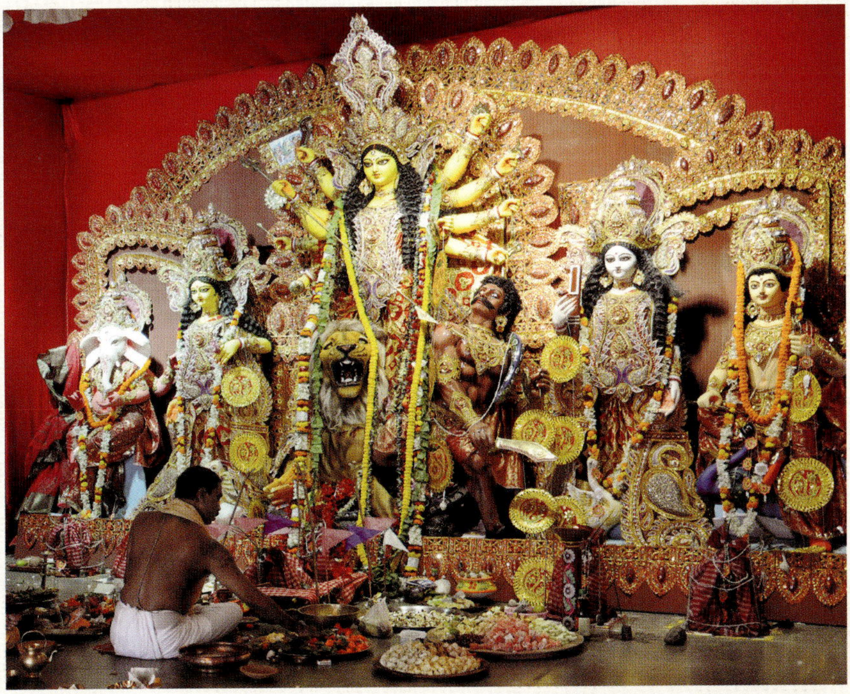

and jollity. The city then becomes a magical wonderland with about 2,000 huge pop-up pavilions called pandals, of varied designs, adorning its streets, lanes, avenues and parks for the mass worship of Goddess Durga—the invincible. These installations are often themed, depicting literary classics, world events, sci-fi and many more. I remember one with Bin Laden as the terrible demon at the feet of the goddess and another displaying the devastating tsunami tamed by Durga with stunning theatrical representation.

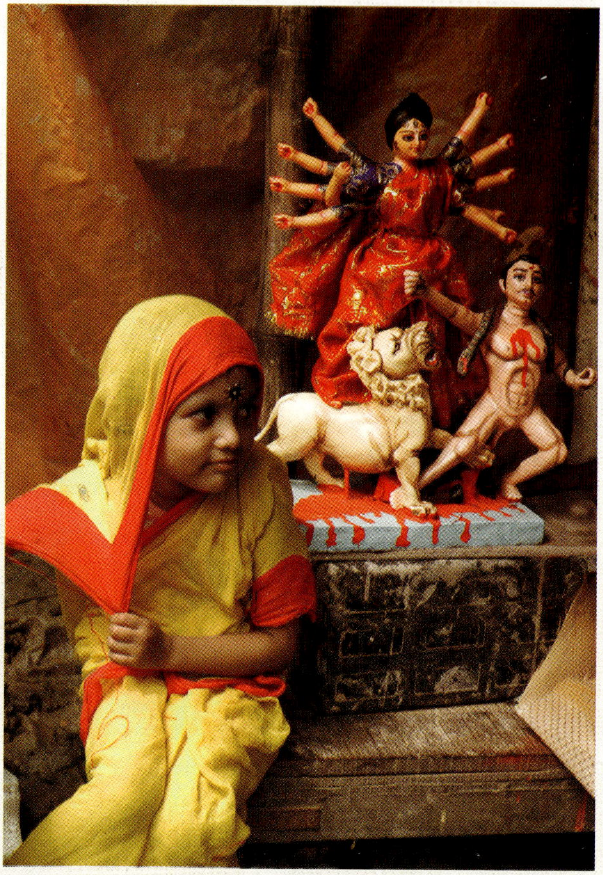

During the festival, expatriate Bengalis often return home, just to be with their families. Entire families dressed in colourful new clothes stay out till late into the night on a tour of the pandals and icons, admiring and commenting on the relative merits of the icons and the artistry of the temporary pandals. Even a sudden downpour fails to dampen their joyful spirits. Emergency services work overtime throughout the period. Eateries stay open to supply refreshments to the crowd whereas offices, schools, colleges and other institutions enjoy almost a week-long public holiday. Most employees receive an annual bonus to cover the festive expenditure. Families exchange gifts. People hold feasts.

Significantly, Durga Puja is also celebrated across the cultural media with the launch of new fashion designs, special issues of magazines, movies, CD and DVD releases and live performances of music and dance all around.

A little girl dressed as Goddess Durga, with the third eye painted on her forehead

Although, fundamentally Durga Puja is a religious ceremony, it is wonderfully inclusive. People of all faiths and creeds mingle well and savour the jubilant atmosphere in and around the city. During the festival, the hard realities of everyday living somehow appear to dissolve into a pleasant glow making the place enchanting. Indeed this annual event offers the city with the possibility to renew itself through energy, spirit and resilience—hallmarks of survival.

Pandal construction is an ancient
craft developed to create huge
magnificent tents as portable
palaces for Maharajas on tour.
The skill is passed on from one
generation to another.

The Pandals

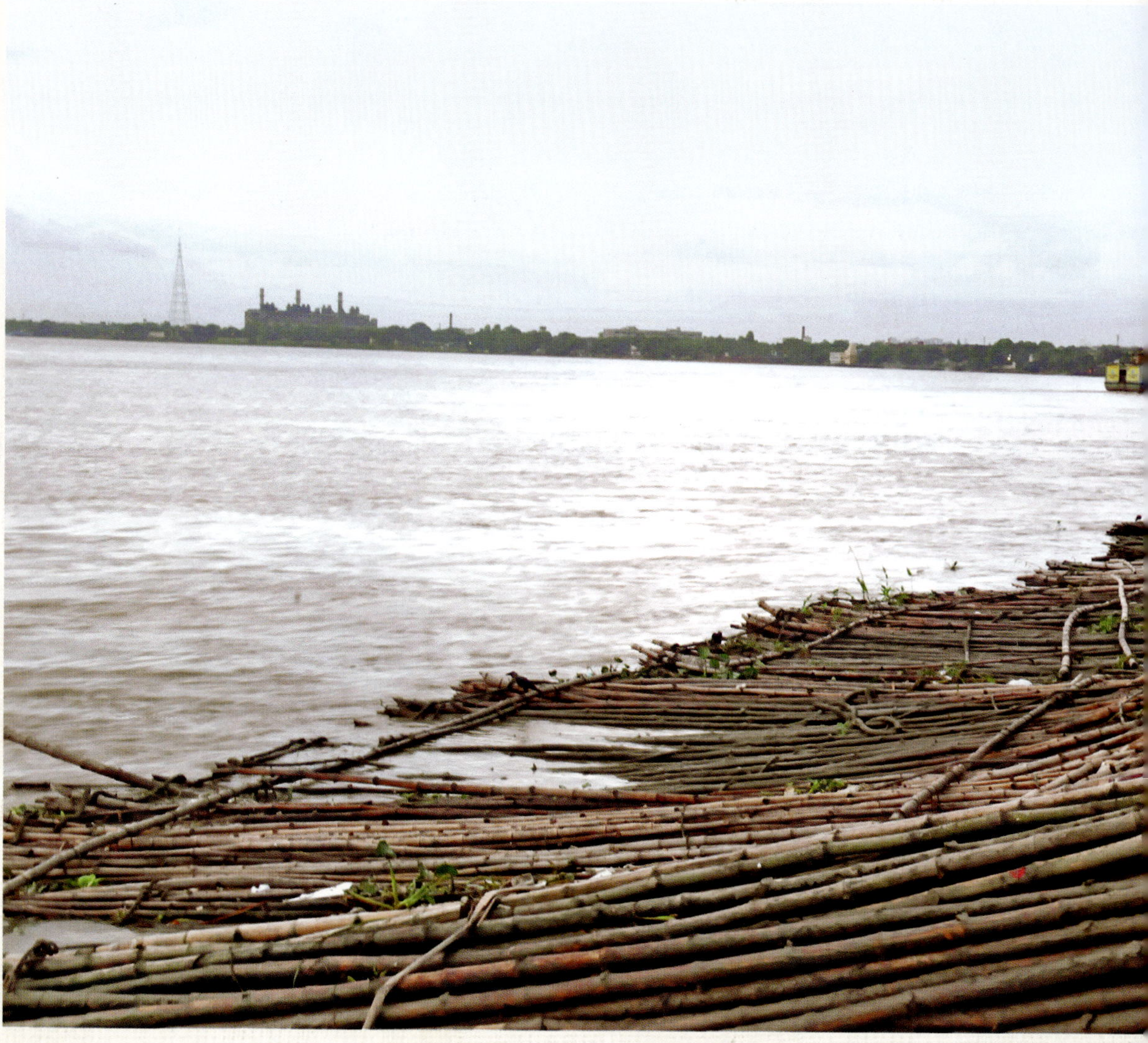

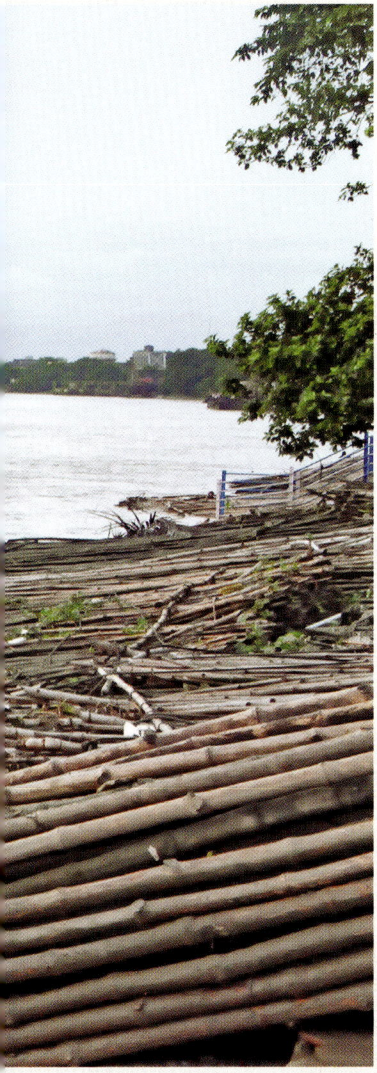

Arrival of bamboo by waterway

The word 'pandal' has a Tamil origin meaning an open-sided shed made with bamboo. The Anglo-Indian dictionary, Hobson Jobson, has some wonderful examples of the use of the word in archaic English. The Oxford Dictionary explains the word as a shed, booth or arbour for temporary use. Unlike many other Anglo-Indian words like 'bungalow' and 'shampoo' it is not well-known in English. In India it denotes a temporary pavilion or a marquee to house religious icons for mass celebration or for ceremonial purposes like weddings and feasts. Thus the phrase 'pandal-hopping' means visiting a series of pandals housing the deity during the festivity.

Pandal construction is an ancient craft developed to create huge magnificent tents as portable palaces for Maharajas on tour. The skill is passed on from one generation to another.

Traditional pandal constructors are known as 'decorators'. They use bamboo, ropes and variety of cotton and synthetic sheets as basic material. Rows of bamboos are vertically planted on the ground. Then some horizontal and diagonal bamboos are tied on them with ropes to create the core of the intended three-dimensional shapes. After that, a vast amount of sheets—dyed, stretched or frilled—are wrapped around the structure to give it the body.

More than a hundred species of bamboo grows in India and plenty of it is found around the villages of West Bengal. The solid and thick variety with close nodes is used to build the load-bearing frame and the hollow bamboos are sliced and flattened to make the wall panels of the structure.

A long-established community of the Dalits, locally known as Dom, are the original pandal makers. Most of them live in an area of north Kolkata, not very far from Kumortuli, known as Dompara. As you walk down the walkways of Rambagan, where sex-workers peacefully co-exist with families and their many small-scale industries, you will meet the Dalit craftsmen attentively slicing and bending strips of bamboo. Stationed right beside the thoroughfare, named after its famous inhabitant, historian R.C. Dutt, they may be constructing fantastic forms like a peacock boat or perhaps an aeroplane around the body of an ordinary car. After rendering the basic shape, it will be covered with old newspapers. Finally a layer of coloured tissue paper and paint will complete the shape. The decorated automobile pandal is intended to carry down a bridegroom to the wedding site through the teeming streets of the city. These are spectacular creations by any standard. Some of these craftsmen even visited Europe and America on commission to build temporary Indian pavilions and settings for shows and exhibitions.

Though this kind of pandal-making is most common in the country, since 1990s, art school graduates of Kolkata and other major cities of India have been designing and making pandals almost in the manner of art installations. These pandals have started to generate and stimulate ideas and debates on various contemporary issues of global and local politics, scientific

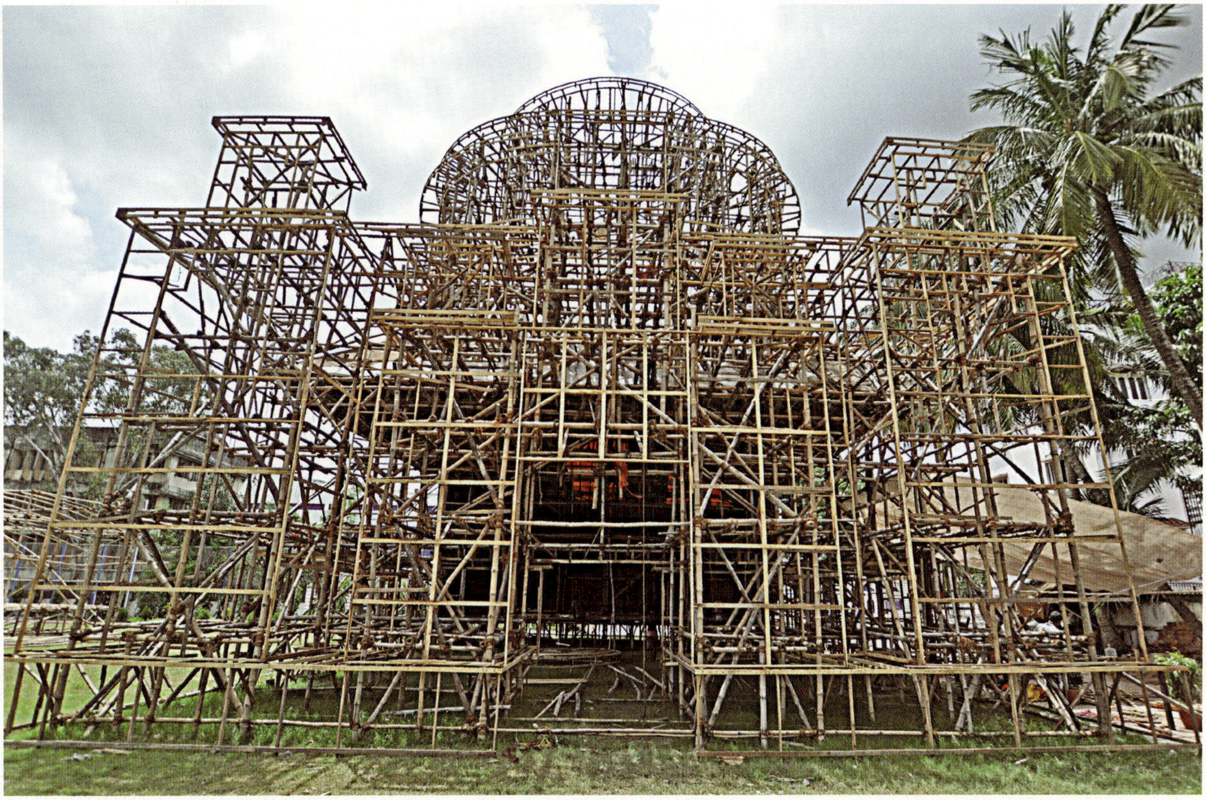

discoveries, imaginary or literary locations and environmental concerns. This manifestation of pandal craft is popularly known as 'theme pandal'. However, unlike an art installation, here the artists do not command a total creative freedom. They comply with traditional iconographic requisites with due respect for the norm of public sensitivity.

For the visual realisation of varied and complex conceptual themes of such pandals, artists have introduced new materials like sheet metal, plywood and polystyrene-foam alongside the conventional bamboo and cloth. Like contemporary architects, they are slowly influencing public tastes.

The basic bamboo structure of a pandal prior to decoration and embellishment

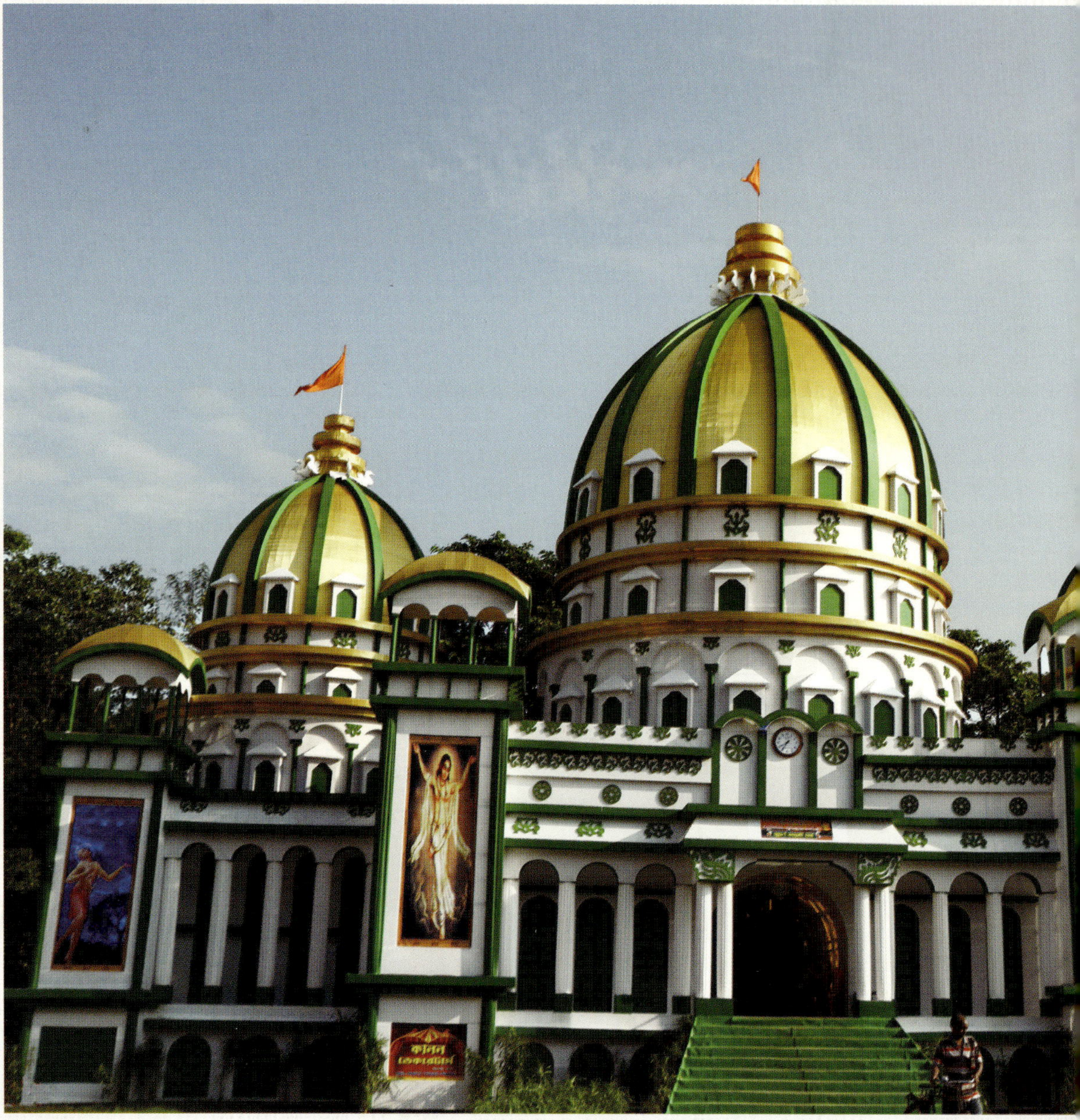

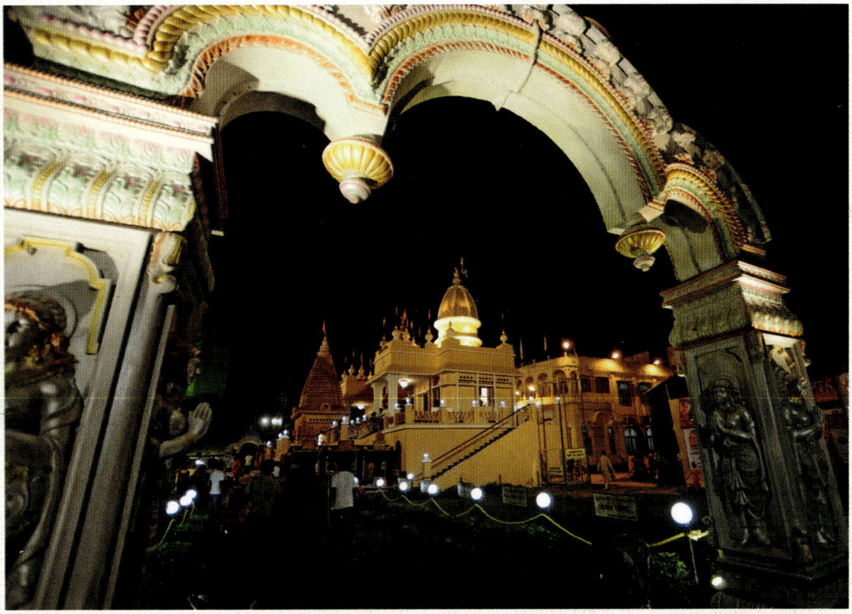

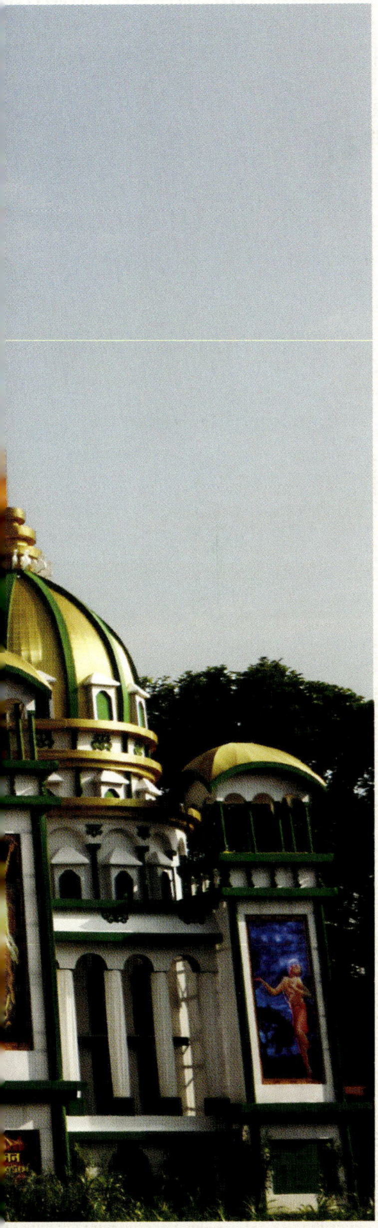

left: A magnificently completed pandal now ready to host the festivity

above: The unreal reality of pandals

Such high-tech architectural pandals are inspiring creativity in individual artists. They are exploring new ways and means of pandal-making. Some years ago, I saw a small beautiful shrine made of simple clay pots and pitchers and another stunning one decorated with folded coloured papers and tons of coloured pencil shavings and squashed metallic foils. The ecological message of both pandals was powerful. The range, diversity, fantasticality and theatricality of pandal art is truly impressive; its incongruity too is often surreal. For example, you can see a Harry Potter-themed pandal standing next to a fake Mughal palace or a Jurassic Park with dinosaurs and woolly mammoths in a

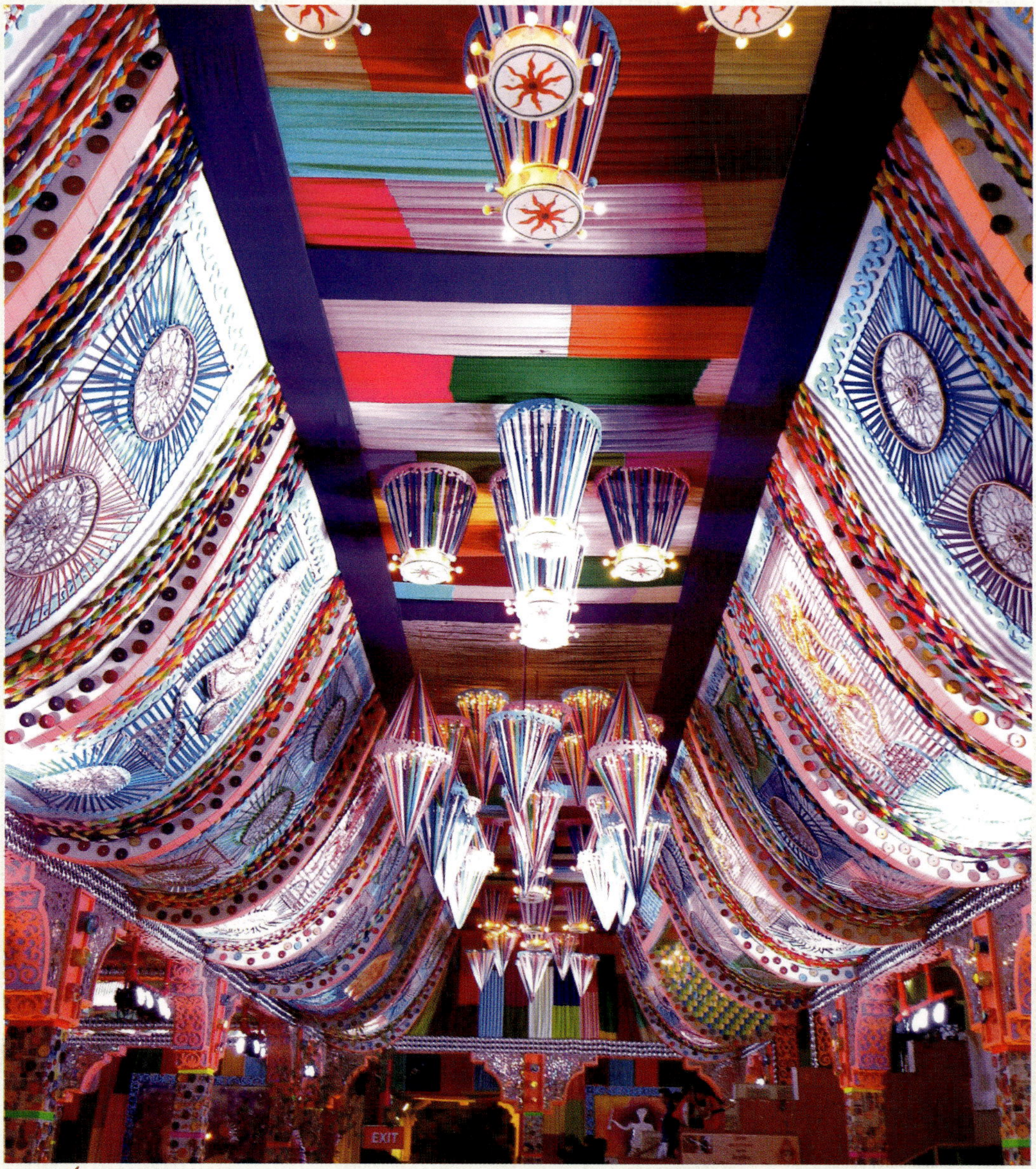

Lighting forms an integral part of the beautification of a pandal
(courtesy: Siddhartha Banerjee)

public park adjacent to an artificial colourful summer bower. The wilder the imagination the merrier the crowd.

Durga Puja, particularly in Kolkata, has always accommodated secularity. The myriad conceptual experiments in the art of pandal building are examples of that. Themed pandals also mirror aspirations, hopes, inclinations and longings of a certain class of people at a particular point in time. They are ephemeral and yet register significant popular trends. These constructions certainly deserve some intellectual appreciation. Photographic and film documentation of the pandals of today are historical evidence of our ever-changing cultural attitudes.

Recent media hype, competition for awards and celebrity endorsement has made the creative burst of the art of pandals a little murky. Nevertheless, the artistic merits of pandal craft and its manifestations await proper understanding.

There are several versions of the Durga story in various Puranas with slight variations in details, but the one narrated in the Chandi section of the Markandeya Purana is generally observed in Bengal.

Stories of Durga, Parvati and Uma

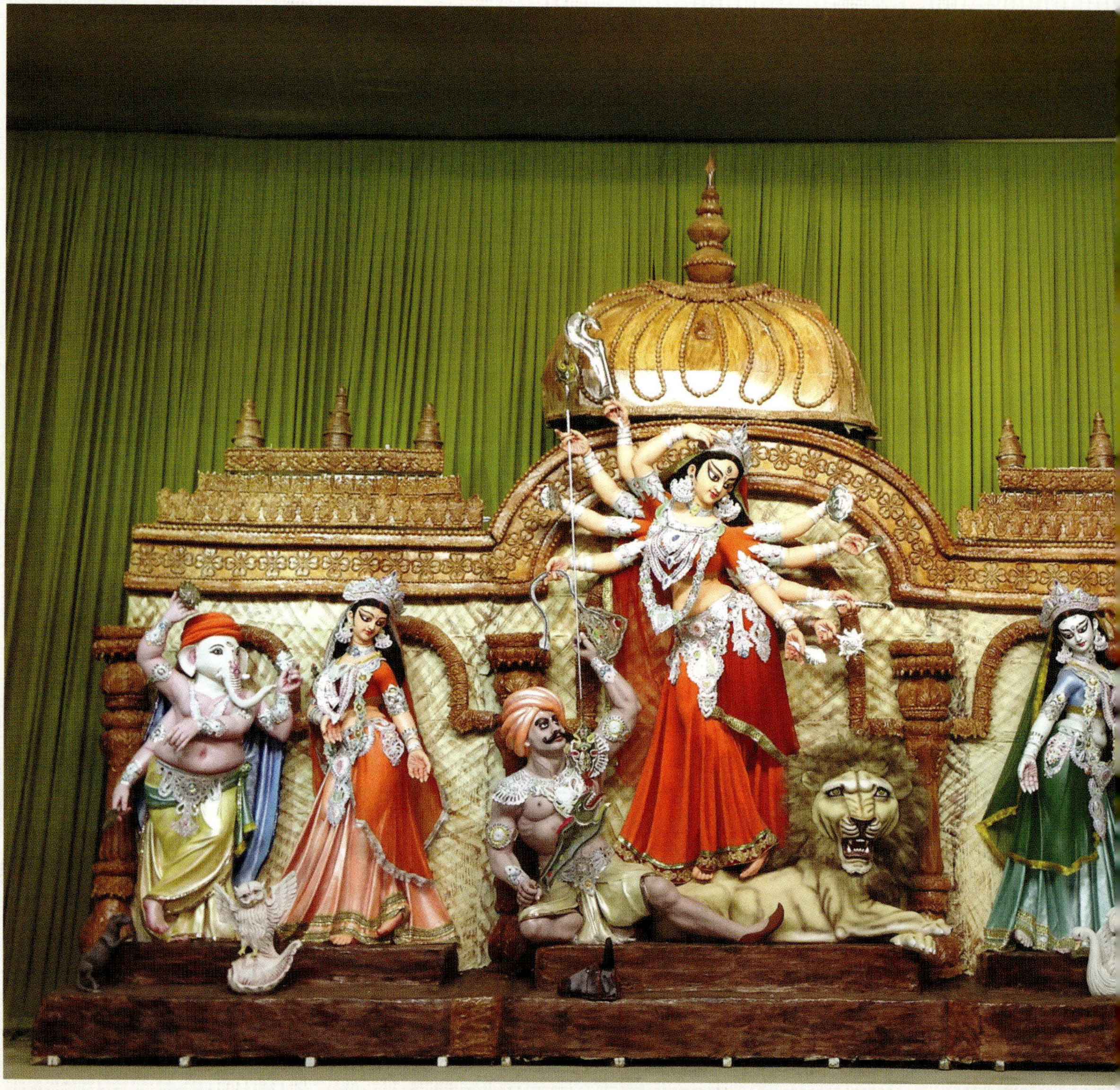

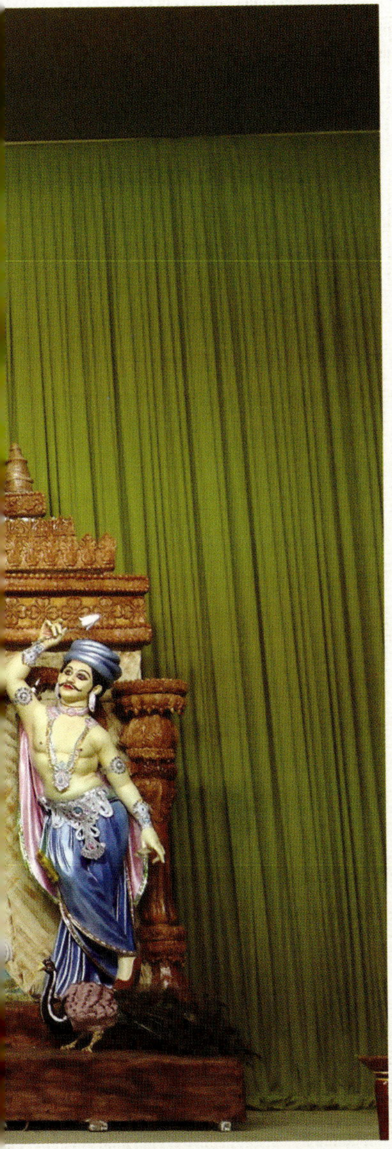

The icons in a barowari pandal displaying humanised poise, proportion and gesture (courtesy: Siddhartha Banerjee)

There are several versions of the Durga story in various Puranas with slight variations in details, but the one narrated in the Chandi section of the *Markandeya Purana* is generally observed in Bengal.

According to it, Mahisasur (the Buffalo Demon), through his steadfast devotion to the great Brahma, received a great blessing that no 'man' (specifically, 'god of male variety') could kill him. Invincible, he became a serious threat to the gods and evicted them from heaven, preventing all forms of religious ceremonies. In despondency, the gods gathered together and sought help from Vishnu, the preserver of the world order. He was so enraged by their trouble that a stream of glow instantly radiated from his face. Soon, similar glows from the other gods merged into it and formed a mountain of glory. Out of this arose a striking female form.

Shiva gave her a beautiful serene young face. Yama, the god of death, gave her long black wavy hair. Vishnu gave her ten strong and gorgeous arms. Chandra, the moon god, gave her curvaceous breasts. Indra, the god of thunder, gave her loins. Varuna, the god of sea, gave her thighs. Earth gave her mighty hips. Brahma, the God of the gods, gave her powerful feet. Surya, the sun god, added nimble toes. Astabasu, the eight sentinels of the cardinal directions of the sky, gave her lovely fingers. Kuber, the god of wealth, gave her a perceptive nose. Prajapatis, the progenitors of mankind, gave her pretty and robust teeth. Agni, the fire god, gave her two all-seeing eyes and a third one in between. Sandhya, the evening god, gave her adorable eyebrows. Vayu, the god of wind, gave her acute ears.

Then the gods bestowed her with mighty weaponry. Shiva gave her the trident; Vishnu, the discus; Vayu, the bow and arrow; Agni, the mace; Mahakaal, the god of eternal time, a fierce sickle; Yama, the protective shield; Varuna, the snake bomb; and Indra, the mighty spike of thunder. She thus became well-equipped to annihilate the tyrannical Mahisasur and restore order.

In Hindu iconography, Durga is represented with a golden yellow complexion and ten hands. One hand holds a spear-headed trident that pierces the demon Mahisasur; another holds the tail of the serpent that bites him. Her other hands holding other weapons, she is mounted on a lion, with the demon Mahisasur tilting against her left leg in a posture of surrender. She is also worshipped as Devi (the goddess) in many forms with varied descriptions and names. She is called Dasabhuja, the ten-armed; Singhabahini, riding a lion; Jagatdhatri, the mother of the world; Kali, the dark woman; Muktakeshi, having flowing hair; Tara, the saviour; Chinnamasta, the beheaded; Annapurna, she who fills with food; Ganeshjanani, the mother of Ganesh. Her other chief incarnations are Uma and Parvati.

Uma appears first in the *Kena Upanishad*. She is the daughter of Daksha, a son of Brahma. The story goes that when she wanted to marry the crazy mendicant Shiva who roamed the forest in matted hair wearing a tiger-skin loincloth, Daksha considered the match with disapproval. But through Brahma's mediation they were married. However, when her father slighted Shiva by not inviting him to his grand celestial ceremony, an upset Uma walked into the sacrificial fire and died in grief in front of others and was hailed as *Sati*. Hence the name *Sati*, which literally means 'the true or virtuous woman' was given to those widows who entered the funeral pyre of their husbands seeking voluntary death.

Uma's death made Shiva mad with grief. As he picked up her lifeless body and began to shudder and shake, the earth trembled. Dreading utter destruction of the world, Vishnu let fly his miraculous discus and cut Uma's corpse into fifty-one pieces. These scattered and landed in different places.

Wherever Durga's body parts fell, those places have become sacred temple-sites for the Hindus. Kalighat temple in Kolkata is said to be the place where the big toe of Durga's left foot fell.

Eventually, Uma was reborn to be reunited with Shiva, as the daughter of Himalaya and Menaka, and became Parvati (literally, the daughter of the mountain). As Parvati, she remains the constant and adoring companion of Shiva. Though she does not perform any significant divine action, she is conceived as the amorous tamer of the wild Shiva. The fifth century AD Sanskrit poet Kalidasa's literary classic, *Kumarsambhabam*, imaginatively narrates the story of their love.

Worth a note here, the traditional *agomoni* songs and the ritual of *bijoya* mentioned earlier as features of Bengal's Durga Puja ceremony, celebrate Uma's brief visit to her paternal home in the plains from Mount Kailash and her inevitable return after five days of adoration.

In Uma's story, Bengali parents recognise their own emotions—when their married daughters come for a short visit from their husbands' homes. The conflation of the story of Uma as a daughter, with the broader myth of the demon-killing Durga, indicates the human side of divinity—the salient anthropomorphic characteristic of Hinduism.

Great riches came out of the sea including the nectar, which only the gods then partook. The first ever kumbhokar supplied the vessel to contain the extraordinary elixir of immortality for the gods and was duly blessed to begin the lineage of potters.

The Myth of the Churning of the Ocean

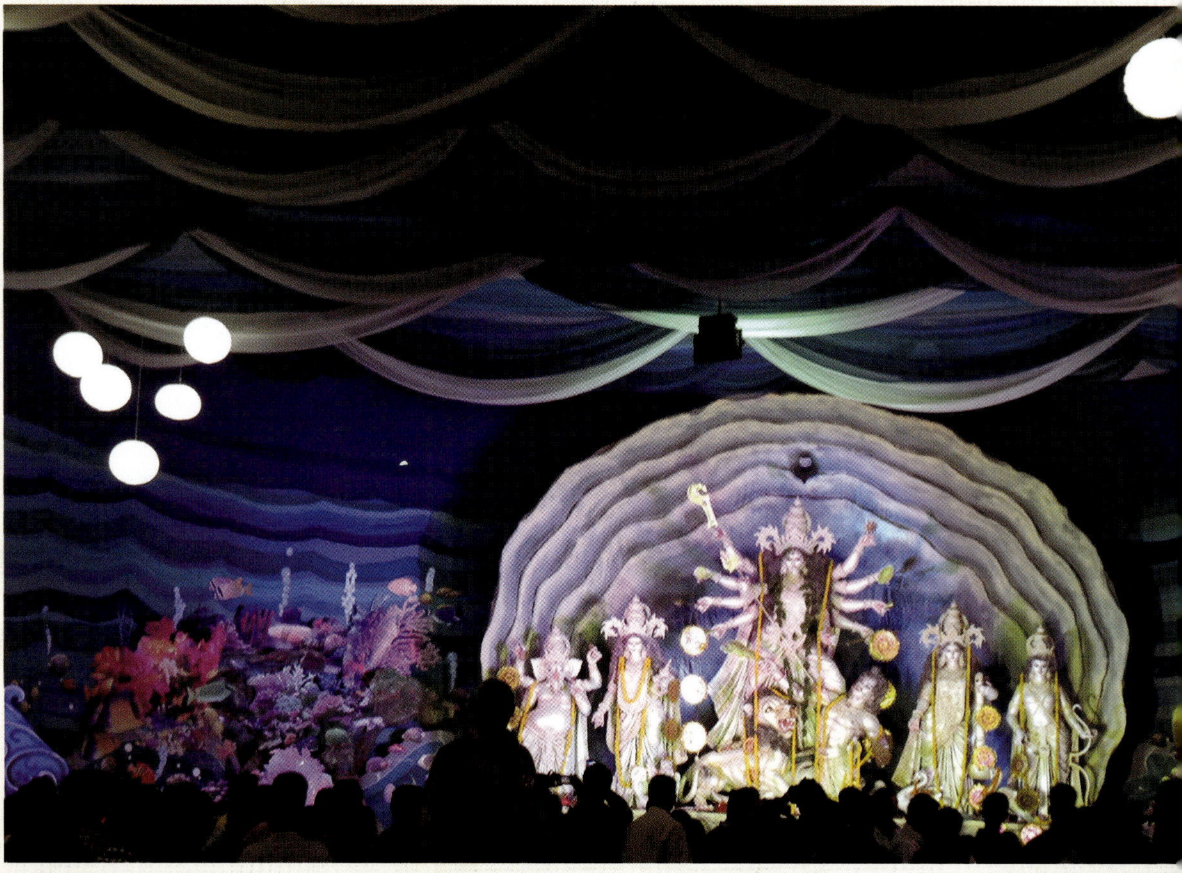

The myth of the churning of the ocean is well-known in India with many variations in the detail. Here is a simplified version from the *Vishnu Purana*.

During an ill-fated encounter with God Indra, the short-tempered ascetic Durvasa felt offended. Outraged, he cursed that Indra would lose his strength. As Indra was in charge of rainfall, the earth became parched, trees and plants withered and died. Bereft of offerings of nourishment, other gods too began to grow feeble. Spotting this opportunity, the antagonist *asuras* tried to take over the world from the gods.

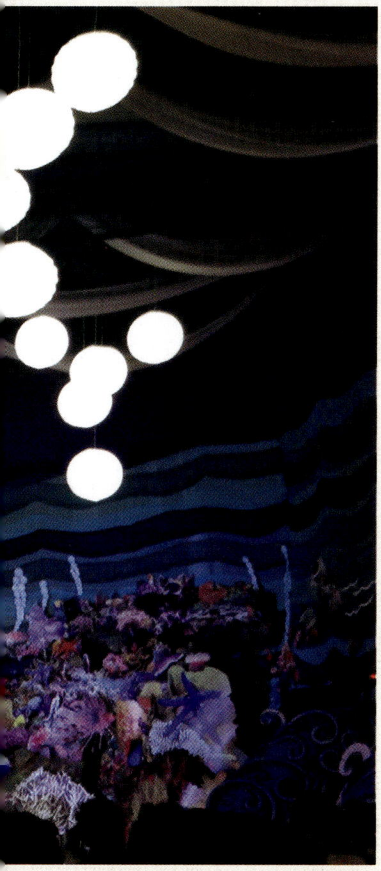

In an aquatic-themed pandal, the icons seem to be rising from a mythological ocean (courtesy: Siddhartha Banerjee)

In distress, Indra and the other gods sought Brahma's council. He prepared a cunning plan and advised them to unite with their foes in search of the nectar of immortality in the Ocean of Milk. First, they needed to throw all kinds of medicinal herbs into the ocean and then they had to churn the ocean using Mount Mandara as a churning stick and the great serpent king, Vasuki, as the tugging rope. Brahma also diplomatically intervened in the disputes between them and made the gods hold the tail of Vasuki. The *asuras* were holding the head. But as the churning began, horrible fumes and searing heat came out of the many-headed Vasuki

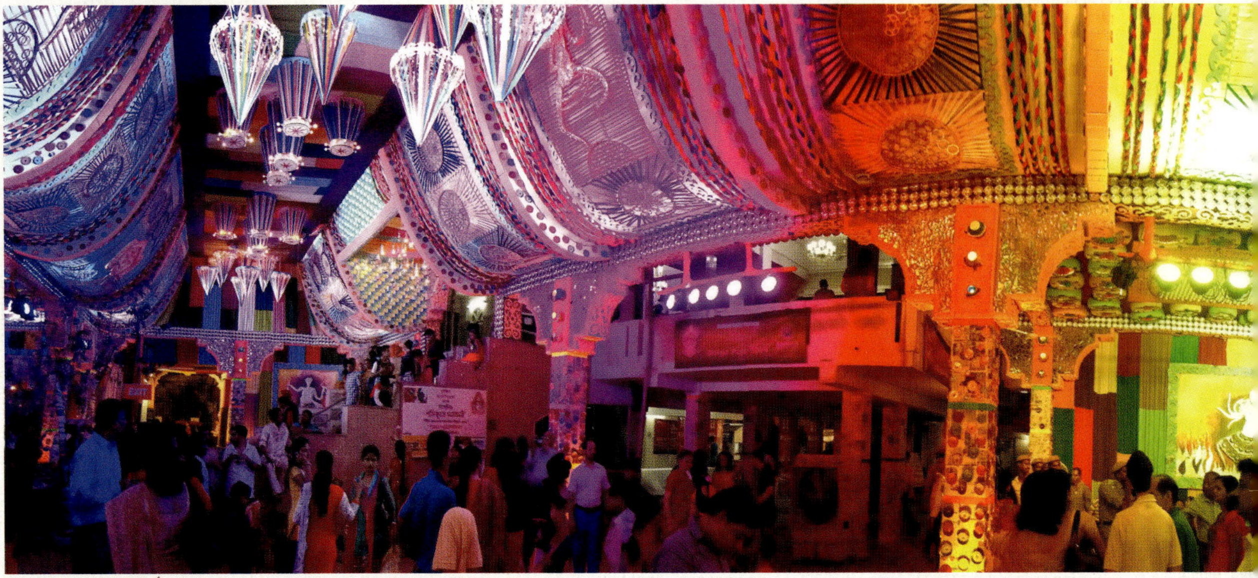

A panoramic view of a pandal teeming with enthusiastic pandal-hoppers (courtesy: Siddhartha Banerjee)

and overpowered the *asuras*. At the same time, Vasuki's breath moved the cloud with cool rain towards the gods to refresh them.

Great riches came out of the sea including the nectar, which only the gods then partook. The first ever *kumbhokar* supplied the vessel to contain the extraordinary elixir of immortality for the gods and was duly blessed to begin the lineage of potters. However, the list of objects recovered from the ocean differs in various accounts.

Here is an interesting section of the translation from the Sanskrit *Vishnu Purana* by Indologist Monier Williams (1819-1899) in 1875 as quoted by W. J. Wilkins in his book *Hindu Mythology*:

> The gods addressed the mighty Vishnu thus,
> 'Conquered in battle by the evil demons,
> We fly to thee for succour; soul of all,
> Pity by thy might deliver us!'

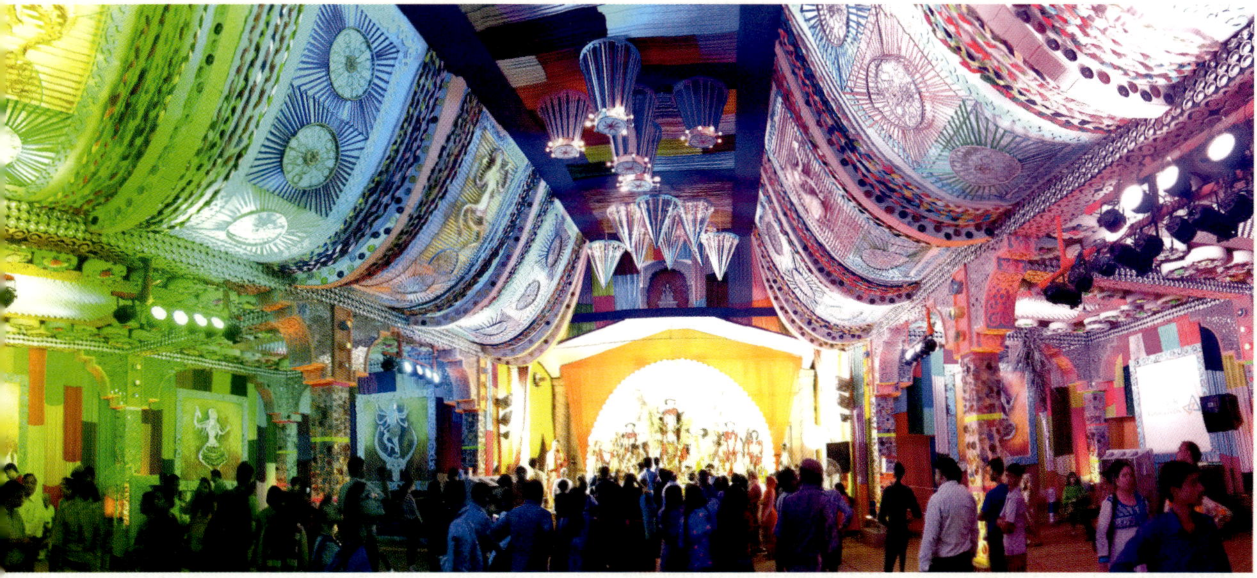

Hari, the lord, creator of the world,
Thus by the gods implored, all graciously
Replied, 'Your strength shall be restored, ye gods,
Only accomplish what I now command:
Unite yourselves in peaceful combination

With these your foes; collect all plants and herbs
Of diverse kind from every quarter; cast them
Into the sea of milk; take Mandara,
The mountain, for a churning stick, and Vasuki,
The serpent for a rope; together churn
The ocean to produce the beverage
Source of all strength and immortality
Then recon on mine aid: I will take care
Your foes shall share your toil, but not partake
In its reward, or drink th' immortal draught'
Thus by the god of gods advised, the host
United in alliance with the demons. (p.109-10)

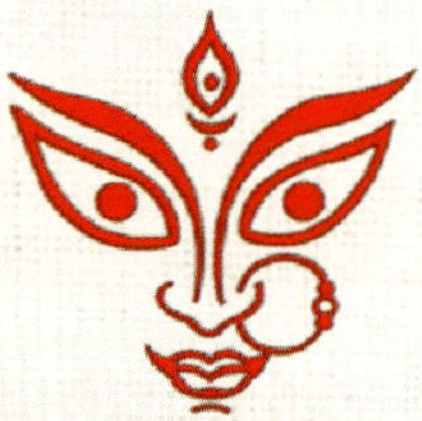

The spontaneous expression
of religious sensibility without
any constraint or embarrassment
is a key feature of Hindu
religious consciousness.

Some Aspects of Hindu Worship

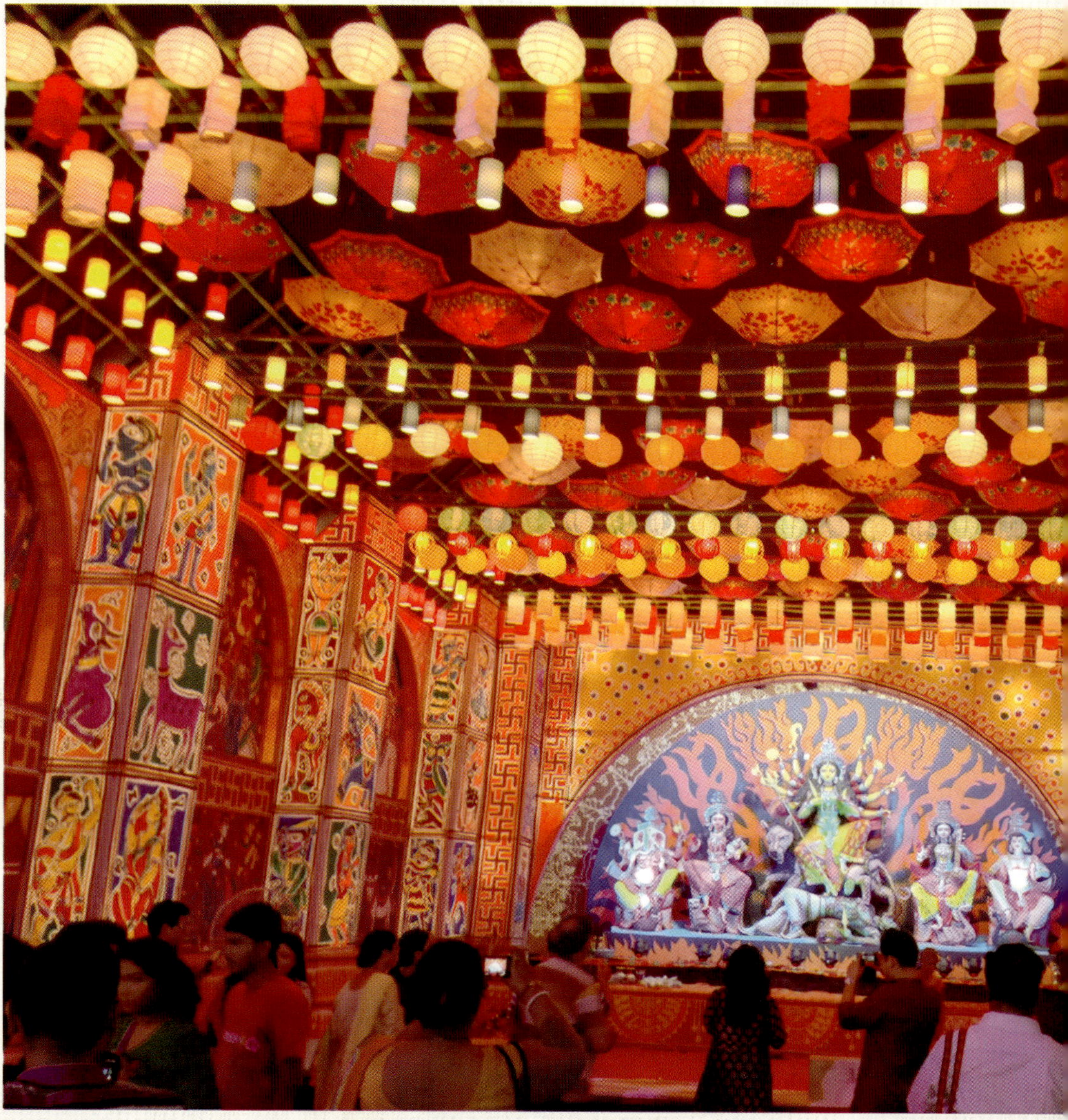

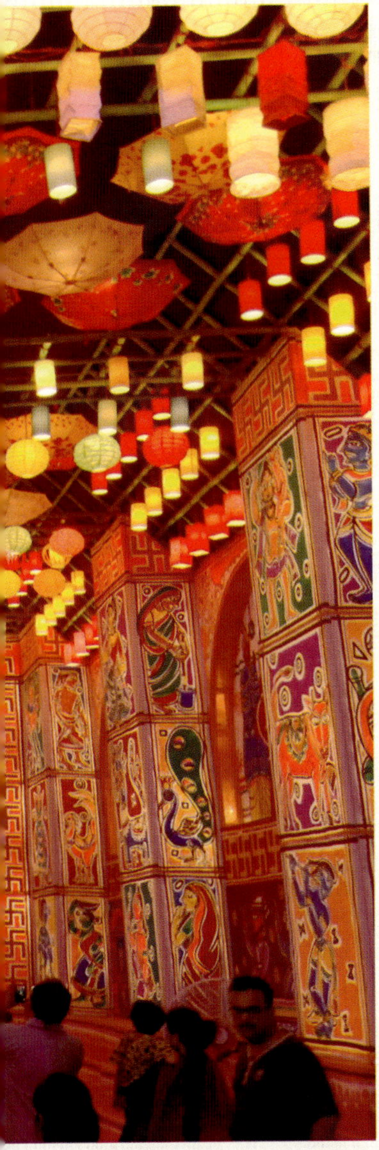

Innovative decorations and lighting inside a contemporary pandal (courtesy: Siddhartha Banerjee)

To a non-Hindu, the elaborate rites and rituals of Hindu modes of worship may appear strange. An exploratory look into some key concepts and features mentioned in this book might be helpful for a better understanding of the culture of icon worship.

From humble roadside shrines to sacred temples, the images of gods and goddesses are much in evidence all over India. Even buses and taxis often have icons of Ganesh, Kali, Shiva and others, decorated with fresh garlands, mounted on their dashboards. Workplaces such as shops or office desks frequently display conspicuous little pictures or figurines of a deity of choice marked with sacred vermillion dots and sandalwood paste. Divine images are also used in advertising tins of a particular paint, for instance, or packets of popular biscuits, on posters and panels all over India's town and cities.

The spontaneous expression of religious sensibility without any constraint or embarrassment is a key feature of Hindu religious consciousness. Hindus love to be close to their gods at all times. They also believe in the presence of the divine in many shapes and forms, including an ordinary piece of rock smeared with vermillion to a finely crafted gold statue of a deity. An essential aspect of Hindu worship finds its expression in an object that personifies God.

Hindus like to venerate a symbol or an image of god. Even in the privacy of their religious contemplation, they tend to imagine one particular image, selected from millions of polychrome pictures, temple deities, famous religious statues and other representations of the gods around them.

But how do Hindu worshippers relate to the mighty gods through such inanimate representations?

They do it through selecting an object, making it sacred and venerating it with total devotion and placing an intuitive trust in its power of spiritual guidance. A Hindu believes that only devotees have the privilege to move the gods through love. They can surrender completely to the will of god, be it the deity Krishna, Kali, Vishnu, Durga or any other god from the Hindu pantheon. They invite the divine sacredness to enter into their mundane lives and alter their destiny profoundly.

To a Hindu, all other honest love or affection we experience in normal life stems from the love of the supreme divine. Such a devout mental attitude is known in Hinduism as *bhakti yoga* – union through *bhakti*.

Derived from the Sanskrit verb *bhaj*, meaning the act of worship, the word *bhakti* is more than a mere communion with the god. It is a complex sentiment, a deep emotional yearning almost synonymous with love as we understand it and much more. It is a magnification of our myriad experiences in a personal love relationship, which enriches and renews us. True *bhakti*, according to Hinduism, brings forth a sense of lightness of being and provides a meaningful purpose to a devotee's life.

However, *bhakti* is not merely passive surrender; it is an act of deliberate submission in search of one's own spirituality.

Immersed in such *bhakti*, a Hindu can bathe a piece of stone with milk and honey, offer sumptuous meal to an image, dance and sing to an icon with sheer joy, affectionately put a *murti* to bed and take the Lord out along city streets on a chariot procession to display. These are all necessary rituals and means to spiritual fulfilment for a devotee.

As elucidated in an earlier section regarding the aniconic *ghot*, ritually breathing life into abstract objects of worship is another way to transform them into divine receptacles. It is known as *pranpratistha*.

Once an icon is ready for worship, the designated Brahmin priest performs the secret and sacred ritual of *pranpratistha*—literally, establishment of the breath of life. Reverentially and solemnly, he wakes the icon's senses of touch, smell, taste, hearing and finally and most importantly, sight.

Eyes have a special significance in Hindu iconography as well as in visual art. Painted eyes can be seen on lorries, buses and boats everywhere in India, symbolising the ever-watchful divine eyes, warding off all evil.

The eyes of the icon remain covered until the last moment. When the priest paints the dots signifying pupils in the decorated eyes of the *murti* with the act of *netro-unmilon*—literally, the opening of the eyes—the icon awakes to receive the veneration.

The carving out or painting of open eyes is the final act of sanctification of an icon, because according to Hinduism, the eyes are the most vital medium through which the deity communicates with the individual devotee or *bhakta*.

Through the final twin rituals of *pranpratistha* and *netro-unmilon*, an icon becomes eligible to give and receive reciprocal *darshan* – literally, the act of 'seeing'.

It is believed that on very auspicious occasions, the devotee may catch sight of the act of the divine glance, which creates a proper contact between the deity and the devotee. This is of course a paranormal experience and an epiphany, and its rare occurrence enriches Indian literature and cinema.

The concept of *darshan* is crucial in Hinduism. It is an important act of mutual communion between the god and the disciple. Through this act, the devotee beholds the deity and the deity too, views the devotee.

Sometimes the icon is made available for *darshan* at specific times and places. There are also rituals relating to the first-time *darshan* of a deity to avert any inappropriate consequences. Often a mirror is used to deflect the powerful divine glare falling on mere mortals.

In the Hindu view, eyes not only see, they are also means of expression and touch. A devotee aspires to touch and express love for the deity through the act of *darshan*.

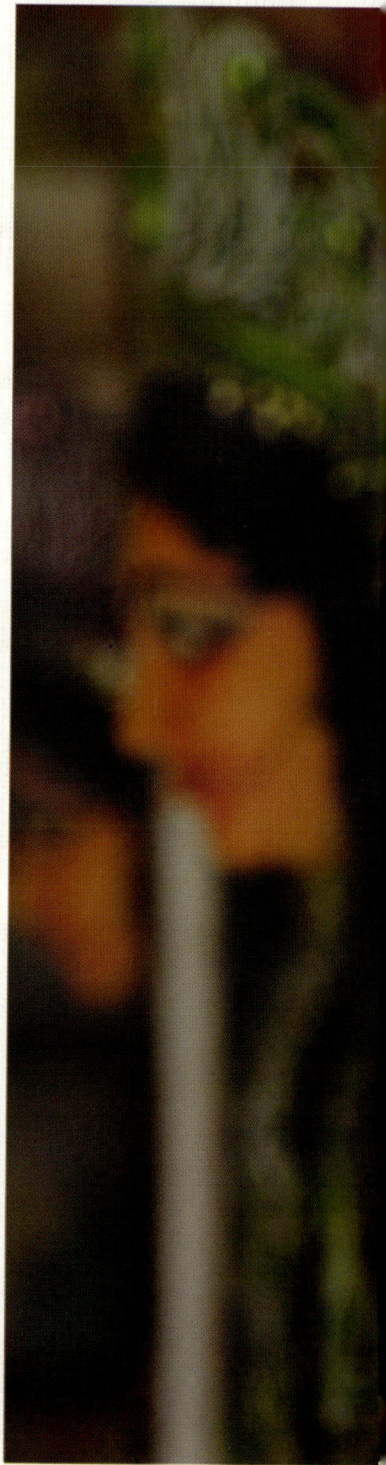

The divine gaze of Godess Durga

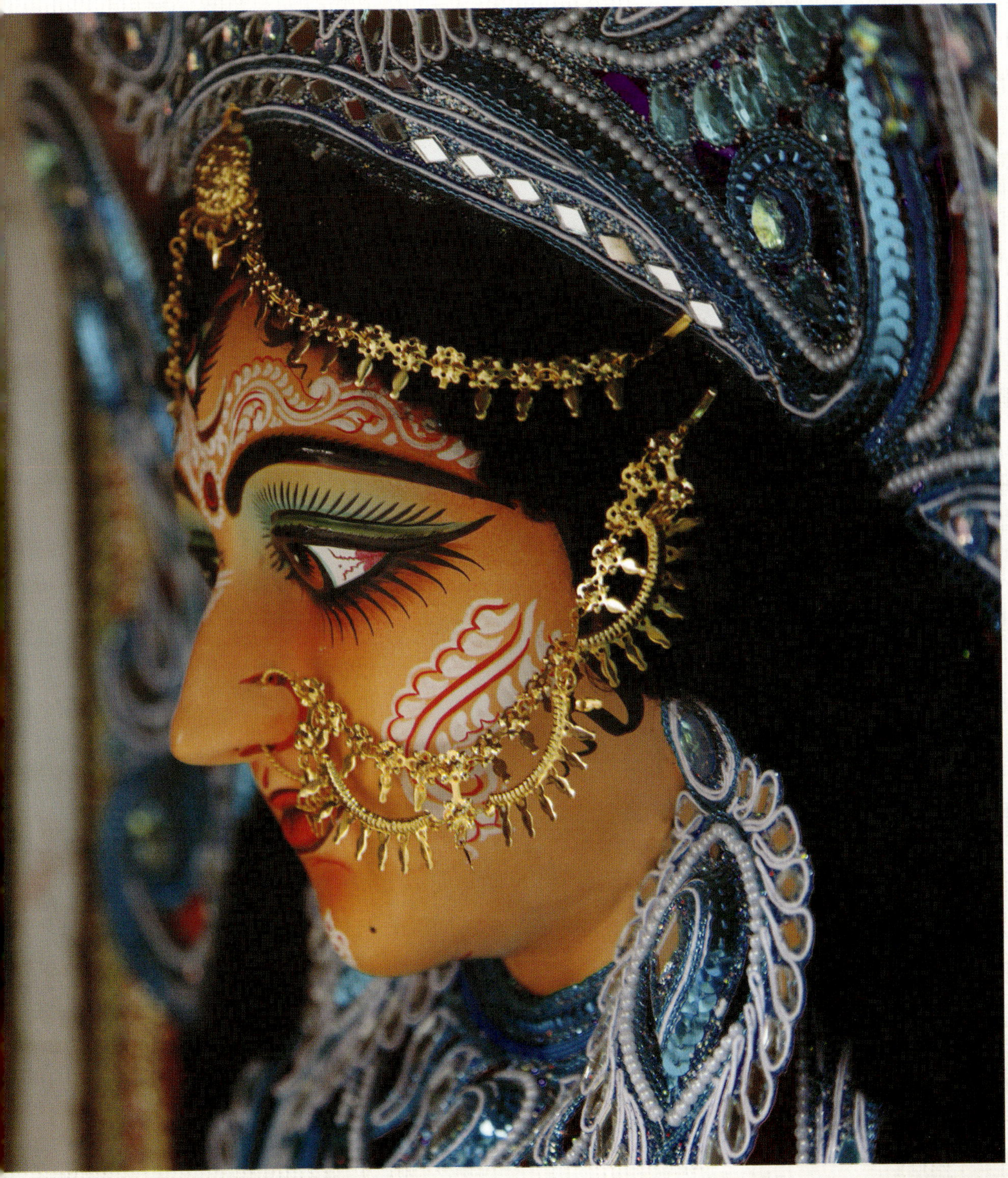

Between August 2006 and
early January 2007,
the British Museum held an exhibition
and season of events focusing on the
rich cultural heritage of West Bengal
and Bangladesh . . .

The British Museum Durga Puja

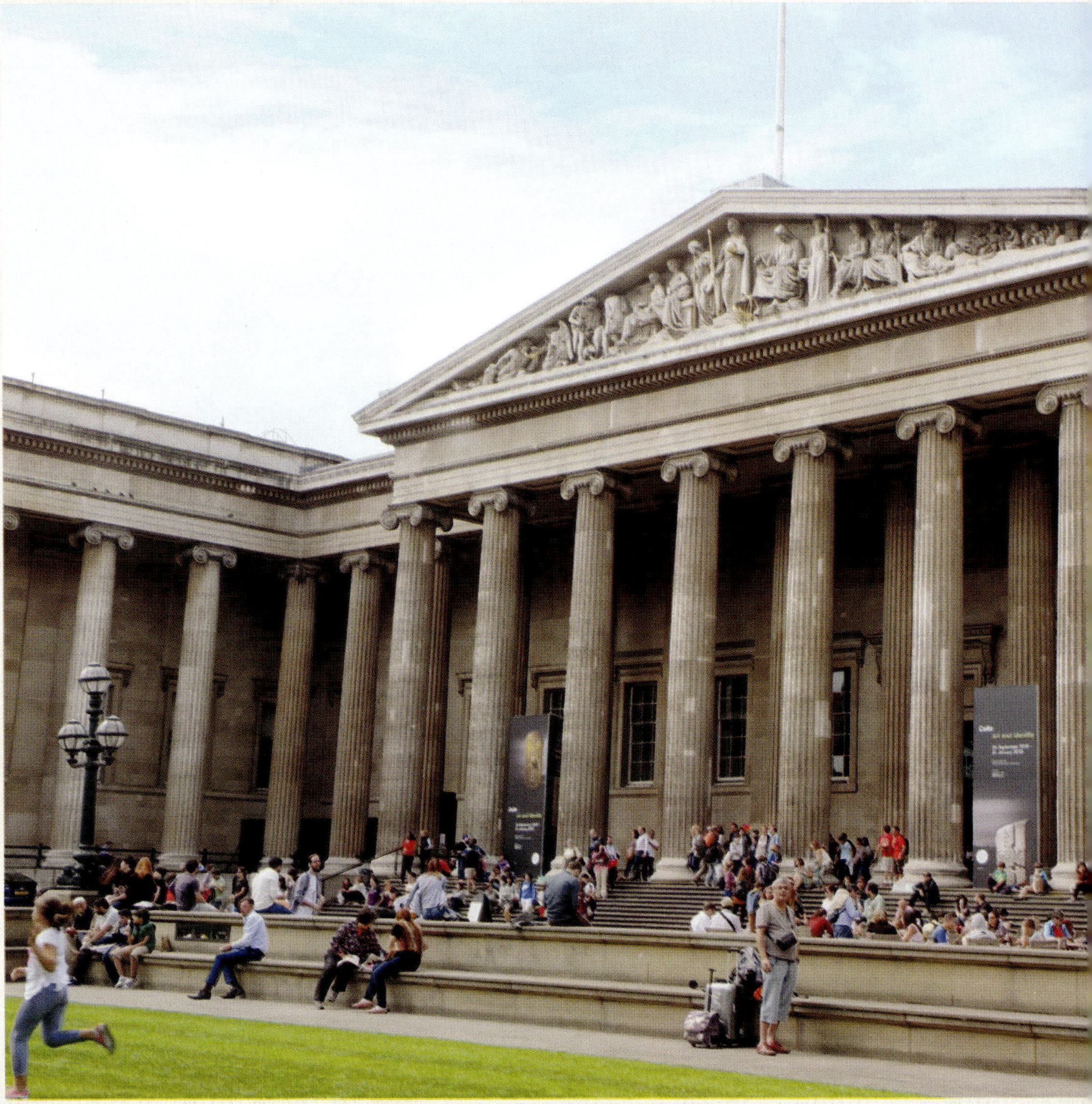

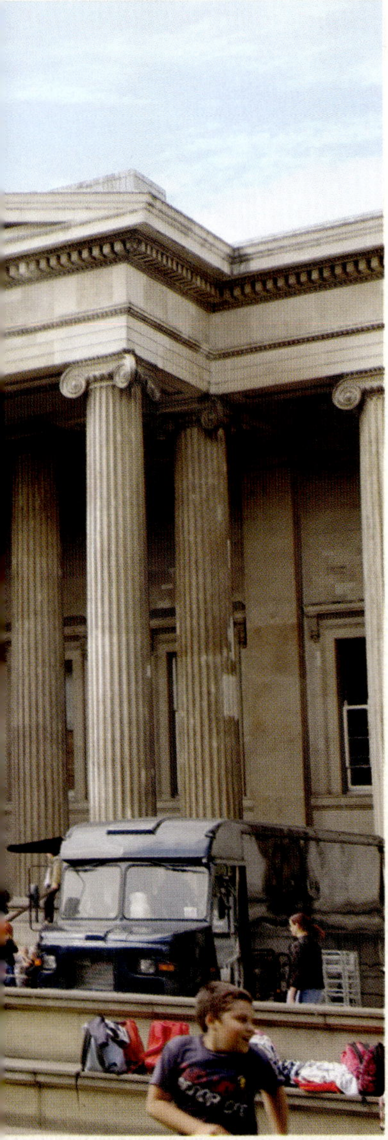

British Museum, teeming with visitors on a sunny day (courtesy: Ariadne van de Ven)

Between August 2006 and early January 2007, the British Museum held an exhibition and season of events focusing on the rich cultural heritage of West Bengal and Bangladesh including the creation of a traditional Durga icon against the backdrop of the bright modern architecture of the Great Court.

Between 12 August and 24 September 2006, visitors to the museum had the opportunity to observe the process of icon-making and the refined artistic skills of the Bengali artisans from Kumortuli. Most of them were enthralled to see master craftsman Nemai Chandra Pal and his two assistants, Biswajit Chakraborty and Madhu Sudan Pal, create the icon of Goddess Durga and her four children from scratch—imported bamboo, straw and clay.

The British Museum, the London Durga Puja Dusserah Committee and the Crafts Council of West Bengal jointly organised the construction project.

After the creation of the image, the community took it to the nearby Camden Centre through the busy streets of central London, for five days of worship.

The icons were then ritually immersed in the Thames by Putney Bridge following elaborate negotiations with the Port of London authority.

It was a memorable experience not only for the diaspora who felt proud of their cultural heritage and helped the museum to conduct the event successfully, but also for ordinary spectators witnessing an extraordinary sight on that day.

Reflecting on the event, Richard Blurton, the curator and author said:

> This was a great activity for the Museum at many different levels. Firstly, it showed the skill of Indian craftsmen who could produce a strikingly impressive image of the goddess Durga and her entourage from very elementary materials and in a short period of time. So many people in the western world today expect objects to appear fully formed from boxes, wrapped in plastic. This exercise demonstrated something large and impressive being made from the very beginning of the process, hand- and not machine-made – and definitely not coming out of a box! Secondly, it enabled the Museum to interact with the Bengali diaspora community, and not just those living in or close to London, but from all over the country. Memorably, one of the Bengali visitors said how, in Calcutta where he was born, he had been used to seeing the *pratima* of the goddess but had never actually seen one being made. Here at the British Museum the whole process had been made visible and understandable to him. Finally, the construction of the image meant that two other exhibitions – one on the paintings of the Nobel-laureate Rabindranath Tagore and another one concentrating on the traditions of Bengali painting and sculpture over the last millennium – could be mounted. These two exhibitions, along with the building and display of the image of the goddess enabled us to present to our large national and international audience a programme of films, music, lectures, discussions and debates on all manner of topics from food to politics, religious tolerance to geology! This was a wonderful example of cultural co-operation, both within London and between Britain and India.

Acknowlegements

My thanks to Soma Das for putting me in touch with the publisher. A special thanks to Upama Biswas for seeing through the book. Also, thanks to the photographers, Pradip Kumar Basu and Soumitra Chakraborti, for complying with my requests to obtain particular shots; Richard Blurton, British Museum, for his generous contribution; Shaunaka Rishi Das, Director of Oxford Centre For Hindu Studies, for valuable feedback on aspects of Hinduism. Finally, I commend Niyogi Books for enthusiastically inviting me to write a book on one of my cherished projects.

Glossary

Agomonigan: Bengali folk songs sung prior to Durga Puja to welcome the goddess to her parental home.

Anandamath: A historical Bengali novel by Bankin Chandra Chattopadhyay published in 1882.

Annapurna: Literally, 'she who fills with food'. She is one of the chief forms of Durga, represented as standing on a lotus holding a rice bowl in one hand and a spoon in the other, serving food to mendicant Shiva.

Arati: Moving a lit votive lamp in circular motion before the deity for veneration.

Asura: Evil opponents of the gods.

Banyan: A broker or a financier.

Barowari: The Bengali word means 'belonging to twelve people' – by extension 'of people'.

Belemati: Sandy soil or soil with silt.

Bhakta: Derivative of Bhakti, means worshipper.

Bhakti: An attitude of devotion, honour and love of god.

Bijoya: Derivative of '*bijoy*' meaning victory, refers to the ceremonies of the last day of Durga Puja, commemorating the goddess's victory and to bid her farewell.

Bishorjon: Immersion. Here it refers to the ceremonial submersion of the deity in the river marking the end of the celebrations.

Bodhan: Literally, invocation. The ritual of awakening life in the clay Durga to receive veneration.

Brahma: The supreme deity.The creator.

Chalchitra: Hemispherical decorative backdrop of the icon.

Chandi: The goddess synonymous with Durga, killed the demons Shumbha and Nishumbha. The origin of the goddess is described in *Devi Mahatmya*.

Chandmala: Wall decoration made of round shola pith cut-out and tinsel, suitable for hanging vertically.

Chinnamastaka: The beheaded goddess. Another incarnation of Durga, holding her own severed head in one hand and a scimitar in another.

Daker Saj: Decorations and accessories sent by post, referring to imported tinsel and sequins for dressing icons. '*Dak*' meaning mail and '*saj*' meaning decoration.

Daksha: A son of Brahma.

Darshan: The dual or reciprocal acts of seeing the deity and to be seen by the gods as a devotee.

Dasabhuja: The ten-handed one, another name of Durga.

Dhakis and Dhaks: Itinerant drummers of large ceremonial drums called *dhak*.

Durvasa: A mythological saint, known for his violent temper, terrible curses and abusive words.

Entelmati: Clay soil, heavy and compressible.

Ganeshjanani: Mother of Ganesha, another name of Durga.

Ghot: A sanctified ceremonial earthen pot used for veneration.

Harekrishna Dirghangi: Famous *kabial* or group leader of folk performing art called Kabigan.

Himalaya and Menaka: Mythological parents of Parvati, an incarnation of Durga.

Indra: God of the firmament.

Jagatdhatri: Literally,'mother of the world', another name of Durga.

Kali: 'The black woman', another manifestation of Durga as the dark goddess, the epitome of *shakti* or fierce energy.
Karigar: Specially skilled handicraftsmen.
Kathakali: A classical form of dance originating in Kerala, noted for elaborate stylised make-up, costumes and the use of percussion instruments.
Kathamo: A framework or a structure, made of bamboo in this context.
Kena Upanishad: One of the oldest Hindu scriptures commented upon by the great Advaita scholar, Shankaracharya.
Kolabou: 'Banana plant wife' of Lord Ganesha; also refers to the Durga Puja ritual of bathing and draping sari on a banana plant like a Bengali bride.
Krittivas: Fifteenth-century Bengali poet and translator of the *Ramayana*.
Kumarsambhabam: An epic Sanskrit poem by Kalidasa about the birth of Kartik.
Kumbhokar: Maker of a certain type of earthen storage pot.
Kumor: Corrupt colloquial version of the word *kumbhokar*.

Mahalaya: The new moon day which marks the beginning of the ten-day auspicious period of the autumnal worship of Durga.
Markandeya Purana: One of the 18 major Hindu religious texts, probably from the eighth century.
Mount Kailash: the mythological abode of Shiva in the Himalayas.
Mount Mandar: A mythological mountain.
Muktakeshi: The word means 'with flowing hair'—another incarnation of Durga.
Murti: A sculpted or painted or imagined form of a deity. An image or an icon.

Nabapatrika: Ritual during Durga Puja which involves a collection of nine specific plants with leaf and branch.

Nautch: Anglicised version of the Bengali word 'nach' meaning dance or a dance performance – a popular form of entertainment provided for the Europeans in India.

Netai Kabial: Another famous *kabial*. See Harekrishna Dirghangi.

Netro-unmilon: 'Opening of the eyes', refers to a specific ritual.

Pandal: A large temporary decorated shrine made of bamboo, fabric and other materials to accommodate and display the deity.

Parvati: Another name of Durga as Shiva's consort.

Pranpratistha: 'Breathing of life', refers to a particular ritual.

Protima: An icon or an image.

Puranas: 'Old stories', refers to the 18 religious texts of Hinduism, possibly not older than eighth century.

Pushpanjali: The act of offering a handful of flowers in devotion or worship.

Raj Bhavan: The official residence of the governor general of West Bengal.

Rama: The seventh incarnation of Vishnu, the hero of the *Ramayana*.

Ramayana: One of the great Hindu epics describing Rama's life, by poet Valmiki.

Ravana: A demonic being and antagonist of Rama.

Samudramanthan: Literally, 'churning of the ocean' – a mythical story about the gods and demons.

Sarbojonin: 'For all people,' referring to community events.

Shola pith: Pith of a herbaceous plant grown in Indian marshes.

Sindur Khela: A specific ritual for married ladies, performed on the last day of
Durga Puja.

Singhabahini: The word means 'mounted on a lion', another manifestation of Durga.

Sinthi and Topor: Decorative wedding head-dresses for the bride and groom made with shola pith.

Sunderbans: A huge mangrove forest formed by the delta of the Ganga, the Brahmaputra and the Meghna rivers as they meet the Bay of Bengal.

Tara: 'The saviour', another manifestation of Durga.

Tarpon: The sacrament of offering drinking water to deceased ancestors.

Thakur Dalan: A hall or terrace within the precinct of a dwelling house, dedicated to worship.

Uma: The first-known name of the consort of Shiva, and daughter of Daksha. Later she incarnated as Parvati.

Vasuki: The mythical snake used as a rope for the churning of the ocean.

Vishnu Purana: The Purana dealing with the deeds and incarnations of Vishnu, the supreme god of Vaishnavism.

Bibliography

Agnihotri, Anita. *Kolkatar Protimashilpira*. Ananda Publishers, Kolkata, 2001.

Banerjee, Sudeshna. *Durga Puja: Yesterday, Today & Tomorrow*. Rupa, Kolkata, 2004.

Blurton, Richard T. *Bengali Myths*. The British Museum Press, 2006.

——— *Hindu Art*. The British Museum Press, 1992.

Chaudhuri, Sukanta, ed. *Calcutta: The Living City*, volume 2. Oxford University Press, Kolkata, 1990.

Cotton, H. E. A. *Calcutta, Old and New*. W. Newman, Calcutta, 1907.

Dallapiccola, A. L. *Hindu Myths*. The British Museum Press, 2003.

Dutta, Krishna. *Calcutta: A Cultural and Literary History*. Signal Books, United Kingdom, 2003.

Eck, Diana L. *Darsan: Seeing The Divine Image in India*. Columbia University Press, New York, 1998.

Huyler, Stephen. *Painted Prayers: Women's Art in Village India*. Thames & Hudson, London.

Gangopadhyay, Sunil. 'Sunil Gangopadhyay jogs his memory'. *The Telegraph*, Kolkata, October 1, 2006.

Hardgrave, Robert L. *A Portrait of the Hindus*: Balthazar Solvyns & the European Image of India, 1760-1824. Oxford University Press, 2004.

Wilkins W. J. *Hindu Mythology*. Thacker, Spink & Co Ltd, 1882.

Index